A Guide to Dog Sports

From Beginners to Winners

Claire Koshar

Copyright © 2002 by Claire Koshar

All rights reserved. No part of this publication may be reproduced or transmitted in any form or by any means, electronically or mechanically, including photocopying, recording, or by any information storage or retrieval system, without the prior written permission of the publisher.

Published by Doral Publishing, Sun City, Arizona
Printed in the United States of America.

Interior Design by The Printed Page
Cover Design by 1106 Design
Cover illustrations and interior illustrations by Flo Lewenthal
Author photo by Angeline Eckbert

"Paw Laws" courtesy of Best Western Regency Hotel, Greeley, Colorado.
First Aid Checklist courtesy of Philip Callahan, D.V.M. and his staff.

Library of Congress Card Number: 2002102711
ISBN: 0-944875-75-0

Dedication

For my husband, Martin
Who is always Best of Breed
to my Best of Opposite Sex

Acknowledgments

On my twelfth birthday, my parents, Leon and Lillian Freedman, gave me a cocker spaniel puppy. On my mother's part, it was a true measure of love as it could be said that she was not a "dog person." From my father, I inherited a love of sports, beginning with baseball and continuing on to a lifetime of dog sports. They convinced me that I could do whatever I set out to do and that it is important to finish what you start. I am eternally grateful.

My thanks to my editor, Gwen Henson, for her capable and professional approach. She has a certain quiet firmness, which I recognize as being useful from my many years as a dog trainer. Actually, this book would never have seen the light of day without the encouragement and concrete advice of author Shelley Fraser Mickle. My thanks to her for her enormous generosity.

Thank you, with love, to my children: Jan, for her unshakeable belief in me; Jonathan, for letting me know that this was no time to take myself too seriously and, on the other hand, reminding me that writing a book is serious business; and Jennifer, for always knowing what I am trying to say and for hearing that which is left unsaid. They are the three Js of my Three J Dog Training School and three of the best things in my life. Thanks also to Tim, Lauren, and Craig for not wondering, at least out loud, when on earth their spouses would get off the phone with me. I never had a shortage of encouragement from any of them.

And Marty, for the cooking duties he assumed, for technical support when I was ready to kick the computer, and for understanding that during this process I was a woman of many moods. Someone asked him once if he loved the dogs as much as I do. He said, "I love Claire." Now there's a man who understands me.

My endless thanks to Sally J. Terroux for her love of our breed and for her friendship and to Champion Bramcroft Dandy, UD who remains bright in my mind. My life would have taken a different turn had I not met them both. To Nancy Nock for her careful reading of my manuscript and Carl Nock for his saber-like sense of humor, thank you. To Ellen Pavlik, whose caring ways touch all of us, humans and dogs alike, and to Pat Tipton for her sensible counsel. Her clear thinking saved me time and energy, commodities that were in short supply.

And to all of my Dogbuddies for letting me share their stories. Thanks for going to the dogs with me. You're awfully good company.

And, of course, the dogs...who come gently into my life.

CK
Summerhill, 2002

Photo credit: Angeline Eckbert

About the Illustrator

Born and raised in Westchester County, NY, Florence (Katona) Lewenthal has an extensive background in illustration and design. She won scholarships to both the Phoenix Art School and Parsons School of Design. Florence began her career as a fashion illustrator in NYC, married, and moved with her husband to Orlando, FL. While raising their son and daughter, she pursued her career as a freelance artist.

She currently specializes in limited editions and one-of-a-kind works. Her innate ability to work in a variety of media, has allowed her to do everything from the design of record and book covers to hand-painted clothing; and from murals in hospitals to china painting and fine art water colors. Today, her works can be found in corporate settings, private homes and medical facilities.

In 1980, Florence became a first-time dog owner. It was then that Claire Koshar introduced her to the "wonderful and rewarding world of dog training."

Why I Wrote This Book And Why You Need It

Look, there is no way to do anything without actually doing it. Your dog might be perfectly trained or, at least, you've made a good stab at it. But nothing prepares you for the terror, the flashbacks of your dog's worst moments, and the stark reality of stepping into a ring or heeling your dog to the line.

It's scary. Your dog thinks it's scary (or worse, funny), and reading this might not fix it right away. At least, you'll know that it's NORMAL (a word that I like to use a lot), and everyone who has competed has felt the same way.

You get to the test/show site/trial, and you've left your dumbbell at your training center. Your shoes hurt. Your boots leak (very bad form at a hunt test and pretty miserable), and you forget your lucky lead.

You are heading for disaster. In this book, you will learn to slow down and give yourself a chance. You might not have a roaring success every time, but you're going to look darned good trying. This is not a training manual. There are dozens of them—some really good ones—but this is not one.

This is not the advice you will get from the rule books or your breeder or your trainer. This is what your Dogbuddies will tell you. One way or another, we've learned the "insider information," and nothing will be better than sharing it with you. We are determined to get you through the worst of it.

When all else fails, remember that your Dogbuddies know exactly how it feels, and, besides, they were in class when your dog did it PERFECTLY.

So, make yourselves comfortable. We have a lot to talk about.

Contents

Dedication iii
Acknowledgments v
About the Illustrator vii
Why I Wrote This Book And Why You Need It viii

Chapter 1. Whose Idea Was This, Anyhow? 1
    Loss of Innocence 2
    Family Tradition? 2
    Friendly Persuasion? 3
    People Who Need Dog People 3
    Blinding Flash of the Obvious #1 4

Chapter 2. From Dogs to Dog Sports 5
    Then and Now 6
    Bringing Out the Best 6
    The International Scene 7
    Back At The Ranch 7

Chapter 3. The Easy Part—Mailing the Entry 13
    The Right Dog for the Job 13
    Be a Smashing Success With the Dog You Have 14
    Before You Enter 14

Chapter 4. Get Ready, Get Set, Go 19
    Six Months Before… 19
    The Week Before… 19
    The Day Before… 20
    The Night Before… 21

Chapter 5. The Right Stuff 23
    Let's Go Shopping 24

Chapter 6. Getting Your Act Together 29
    Planning to Have a Plan 29
    Making the Space and the Stuff Come Out Even 30
    My Dogbuddy Pat's Indispensable Stuff 35

Chapter 7. Taking It On the Road 37
    Fellow Travelers 37
    Keeping Up Your Strength 40
    Riding Shotgun 41
    The Friendly Skies 44
    Home Away From Home 46
    "Paw Laws" 48

Chapter 8. Staying on Top of Your Game 49
    The Doctor Is In. 51
    Short Course in First Aid. 57
    Sick as a Dog 59
    Dogbuddies First Aid Kit 60

Chapter 9. Food, Glorious Food. 61
    What's for Dinner?. 61
    Dog Foods 62
    Kibble Over Canned 63
    Designer Dog Foods 64
    Home Cookin'. 65
    Food Pans 66
    The Puppies 67
    The Grownups 67
    Final Thought on Food 69

Chapter 10. Looking Calm or Something Close to It. 71
    Fear of Failure. 72
    Fear of Looking Stupid 73
    Fear of Not Being Ready 74
    Fear of Making a Big Mistake 75
    Coping 76
    So What Should We Do About It?. 79
    Waiting for the Good Times 82

Chapter 11. Show Time. 83
    Breeding Tells 83
    Oh, Happy Day 84
    A Little Loving Kindness. 89
    Politics 90
    The Plunge. 90
    Kids at Dog Shows 94
    Dog Show Food 95
    Loading Up for the Ride Home 97
    Blinding Flash of the Obvious #2 98

Chapter 12. Love, Honor, and Obey 99
    Welcome Home 99
    Puppystart 100
    Canine Good Citizens. 100
    Take Thee to a Training Class 102
    Are You Ready? 104
    Utility Is Never Boring 109
    Obedience Trial Champions 109
    Tracking. 110

Rally. 110
Obedience Has No Favorites 111
Blinding Flash of the Obvious #3. 112

Chapter 13. Out Standing in His Field 113
Gearing Up for the Field 114
If You Want Anything, Just Whistle 115
Dummies or Whatever Falls From the Sky 116
Judges 117
The Field Trip 119
The Unconventional Wisdom 121
The Work in Progress 124

Chapter 14. A Leap of Faith. 127
Hey, Look What's on TV 128
Attitude Adjustment 132
Basic Approach 132
We're Off and Jumping 135
And Besides Agility, There's Flyball. 137
The Plus Side 137
Blinding Flash of the Obvious #4 138

Chapter 15. Remain Calm; Help Is on the Way 139
The First Step. 140
Where Do We Go From Here? 143

Chapter 16. Letting Go 147
Losing One 148
Will 148

Chapter 17. Getting on With It 151
All Over But the Shouting 151
Applause, Applause 152
Winning Isn't Everything 153
The Dogs 154
The Dog Sports. 154
We Never Doubted for a Minute. 155
Postscript, Surviving to Come Back Another Day 156

dogbuddy (dog.bud′ē) *n.*, pl.–dies

1. a close companion 2. one who talks the same language 3. one who feels bad when you do 4. one who never buys clothes without pockets.

1

Whose Idea Was This, Anyhow?

Looking back, most of us are never able to figure out what hit us. One minute we were going about our perfectly sane lives, and the next we found ourselves unable to conduct a conversation that didn't involve the last show, the next hunt test, or next week's obedience trial. We can talk for hours over the complexities of tracking if we can get anyone to listen.

How did this all get started? Let me count the ways. Maybe it was, "Oh, let's just go and have a look." Or "Wouldn't it be nice to have one sleeping in front of the fireplace?" Or "You know, we had a pug when I was a kid." Or "Little Susie is really afraid of dogs. We ought to do SOMETHING to get her over it." Or "Since YOU don't feel like it, I need a dog to go running with me." Very seldom, my friends, is it, "Let's get a dog so that we can compete." That never enters your minds until later, much later, and then, it's too late. You're in the dog game for good.

Loss of Innocence

We all know that no dog ever woke up one morning and said, "Let's turn me into a hot shot obedience dog. I really like this stuff." No, it was more like your beloved instructor, the best Dogbuddy of them all, said, on a night when your dog was looking at you adoringly and getting it all right, "We really should DO SOMETHING with that dog." You thought about it for a while, and since you had already abandoned hope of playing shortstop for the Seattle Mariners or dancing Swan Lake with the American Ballet Theater, you decided to give it a try.

And that's how you started down the Primrose Path to a questionable life of obedience trials, dog shows, hunt tests, agility events, or, God forbid, all. Or you decided that you were really an exhibitionist at heart and loved feeling foolish in front of large crowds of unfriendly people. Or maybe you just enjoy a sense of danger.

Keep one thing straight; you may never win a thing that some dog hasn't won for you. Now, we understand that your dog would be just as happy taking long naps or getting into the trash as he would walking flawlessly at heel in obedience or waiting endlessly in his crate for his turn in the showring. Having determined that, you'd better spend a lot of time seeing to it that he feels great, because it definitely wasn't his idea.

Family Tradition?

In case this hadn't occurred to you, it wasn't your family's idea either. They will point this out to you when you spend more money with the veterinarian than you do with the pediatrician. Your family recognizes the fact that when you bounce out of bed before daylight, it is not to make them homemade biscuits. It is to load up for the show/trial/test.

Son Jon, one of my charter Dogbuddies, still reminds me that I would knock on his door on a Saturday morning at zero-dawn hundred and say, "Jon, would you like to go out for breakfast with me before I leave for the show?" Being too unconscious to know what he was doing, he would agree and stumble out of his room. And then I'd ask, "Oh, and before we go...could you just load these six dog crates, tack box, grooming table, and four gallons of water?"

Thirty years later, he still wonders if those breakfasts were worth it. The moral here is to be very kind to your Dogbuddies, volunteer or not, who didn't dream up this little escapade but were there to send you on your way.

By now, you've realized that your husband/wife/kids/ partner might encourage you without understanding one word of your exotic new language. Highly technical terms like "made the cut," "NQ," or "blinked the bird" mean virtually nothing to them. Actually, your dog doesn't understand much of it either, but he doesn't care. He just likes being with you.

So, if it wasn't your partner/husband/kids/wife's idea, then it follows that it was NOT something that your mother dreamed up. No, your mother would rather you were a "Friend of the Library" or ANYTHING respectable.

Friendly Persuasion?

Hey, if your family doesn't get it, what on earth do you expect from your friends? Odd looks or, at best, deep concern. After all, dogs are to pet or feed or take out on your morning run...and your little obsession makes it impossible to be anywhere for dinner on a Saturday night. You'll never make it back from the show/test/hunt in time.

People Who Need Dog People

It comes down to this...you, all by yourself, decided that you were a DOG PERSON, and off you went in the pursuit of ribbons, titles, and PRIZES.

Well, all right, we're in it together now. Lucky for you, your dog is willing to go along with the gag. Let me tell you, this is where your Dogbuddies really come in handy. Dogbuddies always know what you are talking about, have nothing they'd rather do on a weekend, and when things go wrong, they're there with an iced tea.

You find out you're good at this. Your dog is good at this, and, best of all, he thinks you are perfect. Your challenge will be to keep it that way.

Blinding Flash of the Obvious #1

- Remember to be good to your Dogbuddies. You'll never know when you might need them.
- There are lots worse ways to spend your time.
- And, above all, don't try this without a dog.

2

From Dogs to Dog Sports

So who dreamed up all these dog sports, anyway? Someone was out for a walk with his dog, and he said to himself, "Hey, let's think up some fun and games for our dogs." I guess not. Dog sports evolved from the kinds of activities that dogs were doing naturally. Picture something like this:

Prehistoric Dog was outside of the cave on a cold night howling his head off, and Urg or, more likely, Mrs. Urg brought him in to share the fire. The Urgs got some rest, and Dog took a look around at his new digs and decided that life had taken an upward swing. From that day to this, dogs have found a way into our hearts and homes.

Early dogs had a career plan. If Man needed help hunting for food, the dog was at his side. How could he have known that his progeny would respond to a sit whistle at a field trial somewhere in the far distant future? When Man needed help tending the flock, the dog was there, little knowing that some day he would use these herding skills to provide his person with a way to participate in a herding test.

The Old Masters painted dogs as often as they did children. The tiny Maltese is seen nestled on his mistress's lap. His job was to be a little companion dog or, maybe, in those drafty castles, to keep his lady's hands warm. Soon we found that we couldn't manage without our dogs.

Then and Now

Dogs were protectors and defenders. They now put these characteristics to use in law enforcement, assuming duties in criminal apprehension and narcotics seizure. Beagles, bred for their amazing noses, can be seen at airports unearthing contraband food products and illegal substances. Some goldens, bred for seeking game, are able to use their superb noses to identify cancer in patients when there are few symptoms. Others are able to predict the onset of an epileptic seizure in time to give warning.

Bringing Out the Best

Our earlier counterparts had the ingenuity to realize that dogs could make themselves useful. They began to recognize those useful characteristics and began to breed selectively for them. With this in mind, breeds of dogs were developed. Most present day breeds are the result of crossbreeding to strengthen or augment those characteristics, and voilà! we have our present day breeds. Form follows function, and the individual breeds became recognizable.

The International Scene

Day by day, dogs became more and more involved in our lives. Adaptable creatures that they are, they manage to fit in in any way they need to in order to stay with us. Knowing that they depend on us for food and shelter, they discover endless ways of making our lives impossible without them.

The Europeans have a passion for their dogs. An English judge lectured in Chicago at a dinner after a specialty and described the "puddings" she cooked for her puppies. We American dog fanciers were filled with shame, knowing that we were feeding a lowly kibble at about a dollar a pound.

The Germans bring their dogs to the discos, and in France, there is a dog waiting patiently under the table at an elegant restaurant while his family finishes an exquisite six-course dinner.

Back At The Ranch

Here at home, the dog is a member of the family. He's along for the ride to the post office. Use the drive-through at a bank in Michigan, and your dog gets a cookie. There are dogs whose most important task in their job description is waiting for the children after school. Talk to the tired business traveler in the seat next to you on the airplane, and he'll tell you about the German shepherd he had when he was a kid. "That was the best darned dog." Remembering, he'll look five years younger.

The University of Maryland conducted a study and found that people who live with dogs are healthier. They have lower blood pressure and fewer symptoms of depression. No surprise here.

I took one of my retrievers to a nursing home for an obedience demonstration. The audience watched from their wheelchairs as I set up the jumps. Before I could get started, a very elderly lady with snow-white hair piled up on top of her head said firmly, "Miss, would you bring that dog over here?" Denver and I walked over, and she took his head gently in her hands. He stood completely still and looked into her face. Her eyes were bright with tears when she said, "Thank you. That's the first time I've touched a dog in twenty years."

This dog was a bench champion with field and obedience titles, but he never had a prouder moment.

Therapy Dogs

Therapy Dogs International certifies dogs for therapy work. These dogs visit nursing homes and schools and bring comfort along with them. Any dog with a Canine Good Citizen title is eligible for the tests. Dogs need to demonstrate a sound temperament and quiet, calm behavior. Dogs who lick and jump on people need not apply. A gentle nature is a prerequisite.

Service Dogs

My Dogbuddy Daphne brought her service dog Molson, a yellow Lab, to visit me in the hospital shortly after knee surgery. I was lying there contemplating a long and miserable recovery when the two of them came through the door. Molson was the perfect hospital visitor. She didn't tell me any dumb jokes about knees; she didn't say, "How are WE feeling today?" She didn't say ANYTHING, but she looked properly sympathetic, keeping her visit short and leaving me in a much-improved mood.

Molson's real job as a service dog was to provide assistance. If she needed to, she could squeeze out the toothpaste from the tube and get the clothes from the dryer. I'm not sure if she could fold them. She was a full-time, twenty-four-hour-a-day, seven-days-a-week, fifty-two-weeks-a-year companion. No days off, no paid vacations. She's gone now, but Daphne's Maggie is following in her dogsteps.

Search and Rescue Dogs

Search and Rescue dogs put to practical use the same skills that are demonstrated in tracking tests. We once thought of a search and rescue dog as a St. Bernard, with his cask of brandy, coming to the rescue on some snowy Alp. Actually, there have been a few bitter, cold hunt test mornings when I would have been glad if he had shown up.

While many dogs have the courage, it takes a rugged dog to withstand the rigors of a search. It takes heart and stamina. It takes a great nose. Retrievers have all the right credentials. Austin, a golden retriever owned by Officer Jim Minton, of Austin, Texas, was a recipient of the AKC's Award for Canine Excellence for his search and rescue work at the site of the tragic Texas A and M bonfire collapse. Austin was a stray turned into the Houston golden retriever rescue program. Canine heroes come in many forms and from some very unlikely beginnings.

The Welcome Mat Is Out

The well-trained dog, like the polite child, is welcome anywhere. I had flown into JFK with Charlotte, a dog who had been invited by our parent club to be part of a judges' seminar. I waited patiently in a queue for a taxi large enough and a New York taxi driver willing enough to take us to our hotel. Finally, one begrudgingly agreed. We loaded the crate in the trunk, and Charlotte and I got into the back seat.

For the first ten minutes, there was not a sound in the taxi. The dog was sitting next to me, but her head was very close to the driver's shoulder. Suddenly, he reached back and scratched her under her ear. "What do you call her?" "Charlotte." So much for hardboiled taxi drivers. When we got to the hotel, he took her lead and marched up to the front desk. He rang the bell and announced, "Charlotte is here for her room." Charlotte's good manners had won her another conquest.

Let Me Entertain You

From Lassie and Rin Tin Tin to Hooch (Turner's partner), dogs have been entertaining us. Sometimes, much to the dismay of serious dog fanciers, breeds become an overnight sensation. Just because a member of that breed appeared in a movie or television show, every family has to have one, and there are the Cruella

DeVilles of this world ready to supply them. Unsuitable dogs end up in unsuitable hands, and we've got trouble in River City.

The comics would never be the same without Snoopy and Marmaduke and Fred Basset. We recognize our own dogs in them.

Dogs on the Sales Team

Sophisticated Madison Avenue advertising agencies design million-dollar campaigns, totally based on the appeal of dogs. My all time favorite was an ad showing a beautiful retriever modeling a forty-five thousand dollar diamond necklace by Arpel and Van Cleef. I'm not sure which was more impressive, the dog or the necklace.

TV ads feature dogs that can recommend tacos and bring the right beer from the refrigerator. Sporting goods catalogs are made more appealing by picturing a good-looking Labrador or golden. They lend a sort of outdoorsy look to those glossy pages. In high fashion ads, the chic model is shown with her haute couture borzoi. They are both looking down their noses.

Maybe your dog has a glamorous career ahead of her. Just think; you could be your dog's agent.

Kids and Dogs

Kids and dogs are a natural combination, like peanut butter and jelly. The dog that goes along to meet the school bus is just plain glad to see his young owner. "Wow," the dog thinks, "I thought you'd never get home." No wonder kids like dogs. They never ask, "How did you do on your spelling test?" or say, "As soon as you get home, I want you to clean your room."

It's hard to feel lonely when you've got your dog with you. And when you want to play, the dog is never too tired or has to pay the bills now.

Dogs and kids have a natural affinity for one another. They can learn from one another. Manners. Responsibility. Compassion. Loyalty.

My granddaughter Jessica, a third generation Dogbuddy, has a constant friend in her dog Rusty, a Shetland sheepdog. She can count on him. He is always glad to see her, likes any snack she gives him, and thinks that all of her clothes are cool. She can tell him a secret and KNOW that he will never tell. You can't have too many friends like that. She is lucky to have him, and, on the other paw, he's a lucky dog, too. Jessica has just the right touch with a dog. She comes by it naturally. Maybe it's in the genes.

In an interview with the newspaper, I was asked about my credentials for teaching dog training. I explained that I was educated to teach school and that I had trained dogs all my life. "Oh," said the reporter, thinking he had an interesting angle, "You'd rather teach dogs than kids?" "No, I'd rather teach kids with dogs." And I would. In dog training classes, kids pay attention, don't have a bunch of preconceived notions about dog training, and understand the concept of homework. What could be better?

Every Day Sports

So, in a somewhat indirect line, Dog went from a nice warm corner of the cave through some interesting developments that made him useful to Man, and from there he was launched into the spotlight of competitive sports.

As far as a puppy is concerned, everything you do with him is a dog sport. Some of it is just for fun, some of it is practical, and some of it has a life and death purpose.

Spend any amount of time with your puppy, and he is learning. You'd rather he kept his paws off you. He gets the cookie for NOT jumping. You didn't correct him for jumping. You taught him to sit instead. He learns that human flesh is not food and he needs to be very, very careful. His human has the most fragile skin, not a bit like his littermates. He really doesn't want to cause you any harm, so he learns to treat you very gently. You are his person, and it is respectful to allow you to walk through the door first— safer, too. He comes when he is called, too. Now that's a smart thing to do.

Day by day he learns useful basics, and day by day his bond with you is stronger. All of this basic training is the foundation for the dog sports that you just can't resist.

So you show your dog, and because there's more to life than just the showring, you try obedience or hunt tests. Or you think your dog is really destined for agility. Your dog is ready, you've thought of everything, and your attitude is so upbeat you could be giving the Positive Thinking Seminar. But let's look ahead to the possibilities. This is the real world, and every once in a while things don't work out. I know it's hard to take, but stay with me and we'll think of a way to get through the worst of it.

3

The Easy Part—Mailing the Entry

All right, your dog really looks good. His recall is fast, and his sits are straight. He's in great coat. He can do a triple, and all he needs are back-to-back singles; he loves the A-frame. He's ready for a show/hunt test/obedience trial/agility test. He is ready for anything, and, besides, your Dogbuddies want you along for the ride. Let's enter him. Great idea, but let's take one last look before it's too late. After all, we would hate to rush into things; there are some basics to consider.

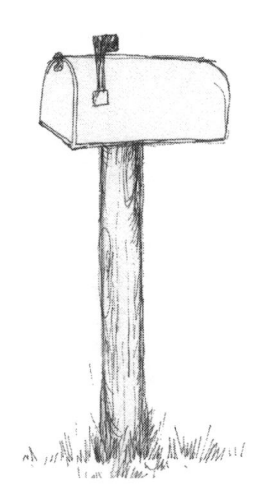

The Right Dog for the Job

In choosing your puppy, you may have conducted research that would make a Harvard professor proud. You may have selected the perfect puppy from an established and reputable breeder. You have even managed to find a breeder who has the uncanny ability to understand what you want to do with this dog for the next twelve or so years. Your puppy was bred for the kind of dog activities in which you are planning to participate.

Dogs in his pedigree, for heaven only knows how far back, have been standouts in those areas. There are ribbons and titles to prove it. Your puppy's conformation and talents have been evaluated, and he is the Perfect Dog For The Job. GREAT!! Or…

Be a Smashing Success With the Dog You Have

Sure, you may have the ideal breed and dog for the work or, like most of us, you'll make the most of the dog you have. Obviously, if you want a dog to be great in the field, it would be a good idea if he came from a field background. If this is your second or third dog, you might have chosen that selectively. In that case, your dog is a NATURAL. But in the real world, we choose a healthy puppy with a temperament that suits us, and then we find out that most dogs can learn whatever we are smart enough to teach them.

The big trick is making yourself really popular with your dog. This isn't really tough to do. Most dogs will do anything for you if you have a positive approach. That can come in the form of food, verbal praise, a relaxed, happy manner, and a lot of pats. There is no one way for training all dogs to do all things, so it's a really good idea to know what works for your dog. Somehow, it's easier for dogs to learn English than it is for us to learn Dog. But, not to worry, your Dogbuddies will tell you that you are a gifted handler who really understands what's going on with your dog.

You will hear that dogs do stuff out of spite, but, actually, spite is a human characteristic. Dogs do things out of confusion or boredom or anxiety or just for fun. They are really not out to get you. It's just that sometimes they need you to explain the rules of the game. This is where you are at your best. Nobody understands your dog as well as you do. Here's your chance to take the dog you came in with and help him to be a STAR.

Before You Enter

Let's take a good, hard look at your dog in competition. Has his training been thorough? Is it carefully progressive so that you are building success on success? Is he in top condition, correct weight, confident, and ready to do the job? Well then, you're way ahead of the rest of us. Nobody's perfect, but it is a good idea to consider these things before you mail in that entry.

My Dogbuddy Ellen seems to do everything with her dogs: field, agility, and obedience. Her dogs look great, very pleased with themselves and with her. I don't think she does it all with mirrors and lights. Okay, here's her secret. SHE WORKS HARD AT IT. Not only that…she works smart. She reads everything she can get her hands on, she trains with experts who can give her an edge, and she tries hard not to enter before her dogs are ready. She has this strange and wonderful ability to know what her dog is about to do before he does it. You have to be paying close attention to accomplish that. There's one more little thing. She trains consistently. None of this final hour stuff for her.

If you are not sure if your dog is prepared for the event, then have someone you trust give you a painfully honest opinion. Not much feels worse than stepping into a ring or up to the line KNOWING that your dog has never actually done what you are asking him to do. Especially when this is in front of several hundred dog people and a very observant judge. Your dog needs to be able to do it successfully and happily in practice before he can do it at the real thing.

The Pros

Just a word here about professional trainers and handlers. Before you complain that the professionals do all the winning, let's stop and think about it. It can't always be handler bias. Maybe, sometimes, the pros are more experienced, more competent, less likely to take in an unready dog, more at ease, and they have worked harder and longer at it.

Does this mean that that you can't beat them at their own game? No, but if you are going to compete against a pro, you're going to need to look like a pro. This may not happen as if by magic. It may take some work. It may take a lot of work. Before you convince yourself that this confident and capable appearance is impossible, take a hard look at all those people around you who LOOK like pros. They started out feeling as sick as you do. They kept at it, and they got over it. You will, too.

Training Classes and Training Groups

Just as there is no one method that is right for all dogs, there is no training class or group that is right for all people. Maybe you do well with a formal, no nonsense approach. Maybe you do best in a kinder, gentler environment. Maybe you like a relaxed atmosphere. Watch any class. The dogs never lie. If they seem to be happy, are having some fun, and are learning, it's probably a pretty decent place. You need to feel comfortable. It's pretty hard to learn ANYTHING if you don't.

Pay attention to the sound level. I've always gotten a lot of mileage out of a calm, quiet voice. Your dog may not obey you, but it isn't because he can't hear you. The classic example that I use in my classes is this: If your dog is way at the far end of the house and you quietly slide his bag of dog food off the shelf in the kitchen, he'll come FLYING to see if it's dinnertime. It stands to reason, then, that if he's right in front of you, he PROBABLY can hear you. Besides, all those whisper commands really look impressive.

It's really important that the training methods make sense to you. I don't care if the trainer is the greatest thing since sliced bread; if you don't like what is happening to dogs, LEAVE.

If the instructor seems competent and knowledgeable, someone acts as if he is glad you came, and the dogs have great attitudes, you're probably in the right place.

By now you have figured out that your life is no longer your own. Everything takes time, so you'll have to be very careful that work and family aren't getting in the way of your dog training. Having said that, easy does it. A little really good and consistent training goes a long way.

Premium Lists

The premium list is in your mailbox. Oh, happy day! This is the perfect show. The perfect timing. The judges are brilliant and fair and without any question "know their dogs." Your best Dogbuddies are going. The site is perfect, and you won there before. It's in that town with the really good Chinese restaurant. More than anything, you're really, really ready. You cannot fail. Your dog has it together, the stars are in the right alignment, and you've listened to Jane Savoie's motivational tape. Your new mantra is, "I love to compete!" Ignore that pounding heart, and fill out your entry form. The premium list has all the information. READ IT. Fill it out carefully. You will notice that there are nice neat little boxes. If you are able to fit your information in those spaces, you are among the very few. Brevity must be one of your virtues. Get help if you don't understand it. BE SURE TO SIGN IT. See that it gets to the superintendent or secretary by the closing date. Clubs are VERY sticky about this and will not accept your entry if it is incomplete, late, or unsigned.

According to my Dogbuddy Nancy, who has served as hunt test secretary, it would be considered a great kindness to all involved if your handwriting were legible. Spell everything correctly. It will appear in a catalog for posterity *as the superintendent read it*. This individual is, by all accounts, a mere mortal and cannot always translate your scribbles back into English.

Don't worry if the dog still needs just a little more work. Some of the best training I ever do is between the time I mail my entry and the day of the event. Think good thoughts. You may be at the point of no return. Once you've taken this step, your Dogbuddies will tell you not to worry. You'll do just fine. You will.

4

Get Ready, Get Set, Go

Getting your dog trained, having your stuff organized, loading your vehicle efficiently, and being able to take off with your dog in a calm, happy manner is not difficult. It is ABSOLUTELY IMPOSSIBLE. If anyone tells you differently, they're lying.

Well, wait a minute, maybe it will work this way.

Six Months Before...

Know what your dog will need to know. Have the newest set of AKC or UKC rules for your event. Read them, and then develop a training plan. Mike Stewart, a highly successful non-collar gundog trainer, feels that no training is complete until the dog can do it five times in five different places. That philosophy saves you from having to say later, "But he does it perfectly at home."

The Week Before...

REALLY train your dog...no shortcuts. This is going to be your finest hour as a dog trainer. You are not going to miss any golden opportunity to reward all those wonderful things your dog is doing right. You will be glad that your dog's training was built on successful steppingstones. You were never one to go on to the next level in training until the last was fully learned. You can tell when it's time because your dog has a bounce in his step and a certain gleam in his eye, and, no, it's not because there's a bitch in season on the horizon.

You have a PLAN, and you're sticking to it. My husband, Marty, who is not only a Dogbuddy but my own best buddy in this lifetime, says, "If you fail to plan, you plan to fail." Usually, I find that quite annoying, although it does have a certain ring of truth to it. He says this, with just a hint of a smile, knowing that I am the Queen of Procrastinators. Maybe I don't want to peak too soon. In my secret heart, though, I know that I need to train sensibly and consistently and *have a plan*.

In the real world, this can't be done at the last minute. I KNOW THAT. If, after all this, your last training sessions aren't picture perfect, you can probably figure out that it's not all the dog's fault. After all, he only works here. You're entered, and you've made your reservations at whatever five-star (??) hotel was listed in the premium list. You can't back out now. You may as well give it your best shot.

The Day Before...

Run the errands. This means gas up, stop at the bank, (The old adage "half as many clothes and twice as much money" applies here.) go to the dry cleaners, shop for snacks, and load up. An odd thing happens here. Regardless of the size of your vehicle, every square inch will be utilized. It goes without saying that the dogs in their crates will be immeasurably more comfortable than you will.

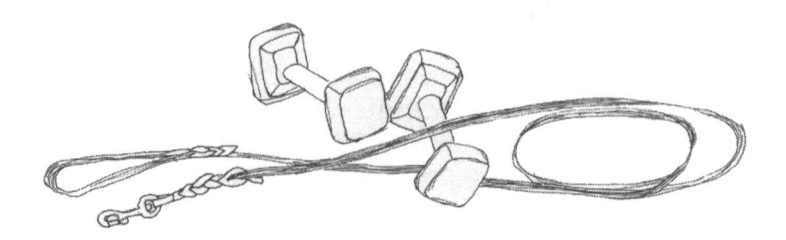

The Night Before...

Lay out your clothes in the order you will need to put them on. You won't be in any shape to figure all that out in the morning. It's a great idea to get some rest. It's hard to be relaxed and alert on two hours of sleep. I realize that every terrible possibility will flash before your eyes. All the books say, "Picture the perfect performance." "Rehearse in your mind the winning run." I'd rather get all the nerves out while safely at home. I picture every disaster and then think, "ALL of this couldn't possibly happen to us."

I do have this reoccurring dream of being late and not able to get to ringside in time. I wonder if someone is trying to tell me something. Maybe it has something to do with that planning issue.

Now, if you don't get all of this done in a timely fashion, neither did most of your Dogbuddies...just remember your dog, your lucky lead, and some Pepcid AC.

5

The Right Stuff

Something happens to us when we get "into" dogs. It is similar to the shopping hysteria with a new baby. There is no end to the possibilities. You need designer dog food, stainless feeding pans, safe toys, walking leads, show leads, slip leads. Short leads. Long leads. And collars, maybe a really nice braided one. Pin brushes, slicker brushes, bristle brushes. Shears—straight, curved, thinning—just the right ones for your breed. Nail trimmers, styptic powder. Shampoo, coat dressing. Grooming tables, ex pens, tack boxes.

Let's think about crates—crates to travel in, lightweight crates you can actually carry with one hand. Who can forget the miles we carried those heavy, wire crates to the grooming area? Over the years, I must have moved several thousand of them, always with great wear and tear on my body. I still have the scars to prove it. One of the kindest things you can do for yourself is to invest in one of those lightweight mesh crates. All of your Dogbuddies will tell you so. And, of course, you'll need crate cushions, rugs, and towels.

Field training? Okay, you need training dummies, whistles, duck calls, decoys, and blank pistols. Plus obedience training equipment: dumbbells, obedience jumps, scent articles, article bags, gloves…and what appears to be a football field worth of agility equipment. You may not need all of this, but let me tell you, one thing definitely leads to another.

I'm not going to kid you here. All of this takes money. Why do you suppose so many of the dog people you know became trainers, handlers, craftsmen, or dog photographers? To support their little habit, of course. None of this is inexpensive. Certainly not. If it has something to do with dog sports, it seems to have some kind of value added tax. It's a little bit like owning a sailboat. If you go to the hardware store and buy a little stainless fitting, it costs $4.39, but if the same sort of thing, about the same size, is designed for a BOAT, it is $32.68. I have no idea why this is true, but the same thing applies to "Dog Stuff." Does this make any difference to us? Probably not. There's something about competition that allows us to justify any expense.

Let's Go Shopping

So where is this taking us (aside from a lifetime of perpetual debt)? It's taking us straight to the joys of the dog supply catalogs, the hypnotic appeal of the booths at dog shows, and, that great den of temptation, the Internet. It's taking us everywhere professional dog stuff is sold. Dogbuddies consider no dog event complete without a visit to the booths.

My Dogbuddy Jean must be the all-time champion of dog stuff shoppers. As a matter of fact, Jean was the all time champion shopper PERIOD. We once went to a produce market and were selecting from a huge bin of broccoli. She took enormous pains to sort through the dozens of heads of broccoli and with great deliberation choose the perfect one. It was magnificent. In awe, I asked her to show me the "second best" head of broccoli.

Jean applied this same perseverance to dog shopping. She was a Bedlington breeder and had the most amazing collection of Bedlington art, from tiny porcelain Bedlingtons to a beautiful gold charm of a Bedlington head study, and Bedlington stuff is not easy to find. When I was buying a pair of ice-tempered scissors or a boar bristle brush, I didn't bother to research it. I'd just ask Jean which was the best. Dogbuddies come with a great variety of talents, and dog stuff shopping was just one of hers.

Catalogs

Put your feet up, take a sip of iced tea, and browse through the dog supply catalogs. This is what you do when you are not feeding dogs or people or working at your day job so that you can take off for a weekend of agility tests. Sure, I know, your non-Dogbuddies are doing the same thing with the Nordstrom catalog or Talbots Kids, but we're talking about serious shopping. If you are between shows or trials or tests, the catalogs are the best place to find all things DOG.

For a while I thought the New England Serum Company was an outfit that sold little vials of questionable fluids to hematologists. Much to my joy, I found out that they've got stainless pans and those plush toys that make that odd grunting noise that puppies love.

I'm not exactly sure who R. C. Steele is, but I thank him daily for his great collection of crates and leads and training dummies, of which I have purchased several truckloads. Without him, my dogs might have had a disadvantaged puppyhood devoid of peanut butter stuffed Kongs.

Doctors Foster and Smith must surely come from the old school of kindly, benevolent veterinarians, because their catalog has among its treasures a collection of dog beds to make any canine sigh with comfort.

Orvis' impeccable taste raises sports attire to an art form. I leave the catalog casually open on my coffee table so that SOMEONE might recognize my secret yearning for an authentic British Barbour jacket. Oh, well, if nothing else, just the sight of it serves to augment my image as an outdoorswoman.

There are catalogs without end. Sporting goods from Bass. Hunt test enthusiasts can be perfectly outfitted by Cabela's. Books, tapes, and videos from Dogwise. Boots by L.L. Bean. *Caution: Don't order everything at once.* Take your time, talk to your Dogbuddies, and find out what you really need to get started. Otherwise, your Visa bill will look as though it reflects an in-depth visit to Saks.

I have been told by a fairly reliable source that I have a tendency to be just a *touch* disorganized. Possible. But I will have you know that I am one of the very few who has her catalogs carefully placed in a basket in alphabetical order—for easy access... very easy access.

Vendors

Abandon hope, all ye who enter here. A few of your more sensible Dogbuddies are going to try to protect you from compulsive buying. The rest of us are shopping right along beside you.

At the booths at dog events, you are confronted with every conceivable dog necessity. The vendors thoroughly know their merchandise and are really good about helping you to make a decision. They are also really good at separating you from your money. Sometimes there are dog show specials, and sometimes vendors of large items will lower the cost at the end of a show weekend so they don't have to load up all those crates and things and haul them all back home.

At the vendors' booths, you can actually see and hold something that you only saw in a catalog or on somebody else's grooming table. This is where you will see, firsthand, the best dog stuff, which you now know you cannot live without.

So, you came planning to buy a nice, practical, and fairly inexpensive lightweight, collapsible fabric crate and went home with the top of the line one with the marine-grade zipper (in case your dog goes on a cruise) and fiberglass rods. Look at it this way, if the dog won, he absolutely deserves the best, and if he didn't, you had to buy it to make him feel better.

The Internet

Just in case your Dogbuddies haven't been able to help you find enough easy ways to shop, consider the Internet. With just a few deft strikes of the keyboard, you can be in touch with the websites of every dog equipment purveyor on this planet.

Before you expose yourself to endless possibilities, it would be useful to have a really clear idea of the stuff you are considering. The best bet is to pay attention at trials/ tests/shows. There is usually a reason why a lot of your Dogbuddies use the same kind of lead. Generally because it works, it lasts, and it's worth what they paid for it.

The last thing you want to do is to show up with anything too CUTE. I am not a big supporter of those plastic armband holders, unless you are trying to save your armband for posterity. That's only likely if you go Best In Show. Maybe they are useful if your arm doesn't fit comfortably into the old rubber band system.

Even your most amusing Dogbuddies tend to take their dog sports seriously. So, while you are browsing the web in search of some elusive piece of equipment, remember to be guided by a certain amount of your normal good sense. If, however, your dog failed every exercise in Utility and your engine overheated on the way home, you may be in desperate need of Retail Therapy. The Internet can help.

You might be looking for a really unique and special gift for one of your best Dogbuddies. The Internet is a great place to find it. My Dogbuddy Donna e-mails me every once in a while when she has located something really good for our rather uncommon breed. She finds these things on Ebay while she's window-shopping. Once, it was a certain sterling pin. I had seen the pin years ago and knew that only a very few were made. By the time I learned about its reappearance, there were none left. So if you really, really want something, throw caution to the winds and BUY IT. I love getting e-mails from Donna. She always finds the BEST stuff.

Worth the Cost at Twice the Price

By now you have noticed that dog sports are exactly the same as any other sports…you need to show up with all the right toys. We're talking about the REALLY right toys. Take the NBA. Does Michael Jordan play with just ANY ball? Certainly not; it is a Wilson. It says Wilson right on it, just so that no one would think it was one of those off-brand basketballs. Heaven forbid. And what about Frank Robinson? He was voted Most Valuable Player in both leagues. Did he walk up to the plate with your garden-variety bat? No sir, he was swinging a bona fide Louisville Slugger, thirty-six inches and thirty-five ounces.

At the very least, you have to show your dog on your Resco show lead. You have to throw your hardwood one-piece competition dumbbell from J and J, or maybe a nice molded plastic one with its lifetime warranty against breakage.

You should have a current copy of Cabela's lying casually on your coffee table where *House Beautiful* used to be. All right. But, why??? Why can't you get your leashes from the supermarket? Because you are looking for equipment that is well made and functional. You don't want to keep replacing it. You'll be using it for a long, long time.

I have two vintage Kennel-Aire crates in my van. They have stood up to more than twenty years of shows, trials, and hunt tests. My new breed champions have ridden home in triumphant comfort in them. After successful water retrieves, they have shaken themselves off and jumped into those crates to have a biscuit and to think about what good dogs they are. Those crates just DON'T wear out. They were a lot of money at the beginning, but they've earned their keep.

If your new dumbbell came from one of the major obedience equipment providers, it may seem expensive. Sometimes you just have to pay for quality. It probably won't split into two pieces on the first throw. It's probably heavy enough NOT to take those lethal bounces into the far corner of the ring (which puts you and your dog in a direct line of vision having nothing to do with the solid jump). It's well constructed and feels right in your hand, and, besides, it's the same dumbbell your Dog-buddy used when her corgi went High In Trial.

6

Getting Your Act Together

Packing up for any dog event can become a monumental task. There is too much to do in too little time. Actually, the problem is usually a totally unrealistic concept of time. EVERYTHING takes twice as long as you think it will. First, there's the trip to the bank and the dry cleaners. The line at the bank looks like the Crash of '29.

When you pick up your clothes, you realize that some essential part of your wardrobe is still home in the laundry basket. Easily fixed…just zip into the mall and get what you need. What a joke that is. Somehow your little time management problem is of no great importance to your salesperson. This person is unable to comprehend why the adorable clamdiggers won't work at the hunt test or why a tiny skirt might not make it in the showring.

Then on to gas up and buy enough snacks to stave off starvation in a Third World country. Once back at home, everything you were planning on loading in a nice organized manner has multiplied, and your job is to fit everything in with a minimum of frustration and still have room for the dogs.

Planning to Have a Plan

This will not come as a revelation to my Dogbuddies, but I did not come to some semblance of order easily. I arrived at shows missing equipment that I really needed. There was no place left to set up my crates except next to the clean-up station. I was tense, upset, hot, and tired. This was not the nice, calm, quiet image I like to project. My dogs thought that something had gone very wrong. They would proceed to fix it by doing something REALLY special like going over the solid jump twice or comforting me by not wasting time on a Drop on Recall. After all, they could always get that drop in later on their rugs in their crates. It became obvious that the old "throw it in the van and we will all get there at the same time" theory simply would not work for me.

I had to resort to stern measures. I started watching the people who were enjoying a cup of coffee when I arrived at the hunt test. I noticed the ones whose grooming equipment was always where they could put their hands on it, and, painful as it seemed, I knew that I needed a system. Does this newfound concept apply to everything I do? Of course not, but a little planning did creep into my life, and it does make things easier. At times I can be more than a little obnoxious about it. I challenge you to find another woman in the Southeast who stores her catalogs in a basket in ALPHABETICAL order. I may have gone a little too far, but I can tell you for sure that you'll find J and J way ahead of Williams-Sonoma. That was my first effort in my grand plan for organization. It may sound strange, but it was a start.

Making the Space and the Stuff Come Out Even

In loading up, people fall into three major categories. First, there is the "place for everything and everything in its place" group. People in this group also have neat desks and throw away old magazines. Then there is the "utter chaos" group. They end up at events just late enough to be in an honest-to-God panic. They cannot unearth their show lead from underneath the rubble and spend countless hours searching for other things they don't find until they are home. In the meantime, they buy a new lead that may end up going the way of the first one. If you happen to fall into the latter category and LIKE IT, ignore the rest of this section. You are truly blessed because you have the unique ability to be able to function in what one of my Dogbuddies fondly calls "organized disorder." Somehow, out of what appears to be complete bedlam, she enters the obedience ring cool and collected, dog and handler well groomed and prepared for a successful day. Don't ask me how she does it. I haven't a clue.

And finally, we have my chosen people, the "middle of the roaders." We were probably middle children and earned our share of Cs, except in things we liked, for instance DOG TRAINING, where I guarantee we got straight As.

Let's have a closer look at these somewhat divergent philosophies.

The Place for Everything Group

My Dogbuddy Carl definitely fits into this category. In fact, he may have invented it. His military career made use of his skills in readiness and logistics. These same skills were in great demand in our local hunting retriever club. Before Carl arrived upon the scene, the club's trailer was known to harbor unidentifiable pieces of hardware and last year's banana peels, or worse. Under Carl's steady hand, everything is clean, in perfect working order, and in its designated place. Are there advantages to this meticulous attention to detail? Absolutely. When something is needed, it can be found instantly, and it will work. Besides that, if you are helping to put things away, you ask Carl, "Where does this go?" and invariably he will say, "Just set it down; I'll take care of it."

The best part of this is that he wastes little time rummaging around and can concentrate on the really important things like running the hunt test. Since I tend to march to a different drummer, I may never get to be as well organized, but clearly there are lessons to be learned here.

The Middle of the Road Gang

If you were reading the previous description and saying to yourself, "Not in this lifetime," then this technique is probably the one for you. You have already figured out that you cannot maintain sanity in total chaos, and history has taught you that you will never have the perfectly ordered closet/desk/van/ garage/truck/life. Well, pull up your folding chair, and we'll come up with a plan.

First, take EVERYTHING out of your vehicle, and start off squeaky clean. A hand vac or a low-tech whiskbroom works wonders. Then, load crates and large equipment, and see how much room there is left. Make sure that your containers for smaller items fit in the available space. My Labrador Dogbuddy Pat, an innovative person, designed something that she calls a Rack 'Em Up. It is a metal rack that fits in the cargo area of a van or truck where dog crates and other stuff can be placed on it. Under it, there is plenty of room for smaller containers for dummies and raingear and that collection of indispensable items that you will take with you.

If you are lucky enough to have a vehicle that the family knows is essentially reserved for the dogs, you can store much of this equipment in it and have everything ready when needed. Wow! What a concept. My daughter Jennifer claims that she drew her first allergy free breath when I provided alternative transportation for her, sans dogs.

Now you are ready to load the last minute stuff. Dog food (somehow, even if you are only taking one Yorkie, it is necessary to bring large masses of food), water container, ice chests, and luggage. A word about luggage. Duffel bags or canvas carry-ons work best. Like a sailboat, a dog vehicle is no place for a large suitcase. If you are traveling with a Dogbuddy, you get extra points for bringing your things in something that can be fitted in easily or hung up.

As I said, I did not come to this naturally and have discovered that I need a lot of structure to get organized. The key here is to make LISTS. I LOVE LISTS. They're a grown-up version of a security blanket. Put your standard list on an Excel spreadsheet, and add things as you think of them. Print it out. Cross things off as they are loaded. Leave a copy lying around where it can be readily seen. Your friends are going to tell you that you're becoming a little obsessive. That's okay. When they are desperately searching for their dumbbell, you'll know that you have yours and maybe a spare because it was on your list.

One last thing: Once you have decided on the best place for everything, try to keep it there. You'll be glad that your dog's lead was clipped back onto his crate after he was exercised. When you need to take him to ringside, the right lead is in the right place. When it's pouring down rain, it will be nice to find your food pans in their designated place. They were placed in a handy spot instead of lurking somewhere under your raingear and behind the toolbox. Store things according to how often you'll need them, and PUT THINGS BACK. If I sound a little like Miss Kettering, your kindergarten teacher, remember that some of those age-old principles still work.

My Dogbuddy Pat, of Rack 'Em Up fame, is one of the most practical people I know. Maybe it comes from raising three boys…maybe she was born that way. I don't know. But I do know this; if there is a sensible way of doing something, she has it figured out. If you find yourself at a hunt test and you desperately need a piece of string or a safety pin or a Phillips head screwdriver, go find Pat. She'll say, "Oh, yes, I think I have one in my van." She does. We were setting up our team's area for a statewide obedience competition. The only place I could put up a banner was on the metal interior wall. Tape wouldn't hold it. "Oh, yes, I think I have something in my van," Pat said, and twelve seconds later she came back with a plastic hook with a magnetic back. I've been trying to stump her ever since.

It Goes Without Saying

I don't know about you, but every time I hear, "It goes without saying," it is followed by some profound truth that has absolutely never occurred to me before that moment. This is a great time for us to share a few of these. Stop me if you've heard this one.

Transportation

You can make your dog trips a lot less challenging if you start out with reliable transportation. We can't all have late model, high-end vehicles, but if you're planning a trip of any distance, it would be an excellent idea to have a good, sensible auto mechanic on your side. Stop ignoring all those odd little noises, and GET IT FIXED! If your transmission falls off on the way to Nowhere, New Mexico, a quick call to *Car Talk* probably won't fix it.

There is nothing much more hopeless than being stranded at the side of the road, your vehicle loaded to the rafters and no help on the way. These disasters never occur within sight of a service station. Even if one does, it will be a 7-11, pump your own gas, and the only person around to give you any advice will be a kid who stopped by to get air for his bike tire.

Here is a simple fact. Repairs take time, and, in case we hadn't noticed, time is money. Both of these seem to be in short supply on the way to a show/trial/test. Obviously, the best-case scenario is to have your truck or van maintained in perfect condition. Failing that, at least give yourself the peace of mind that comes with having it checked out before you leave.

When that blessed time arrives for you to be purchasing a new or used vehicle, make sure that all those items you already own fit into it. After the purchase is usually not a good time to discover that there isn't enough room for your brand new crates.

If you are buying a used car or truck, pray that it was pre-owned by someone like my Dogbuddy Carl. His cast-offs look better than my van did when it was rolling out of the showroom.

Out of Chaos Comes Order

You've got everything loaded. You've double-checked your Master List one last time. Everything is shipshape, and you feel righteous. You should. You may not always be a mass of organization so, if you fall back on your old ways and can't find your best thinning shears, well, that's what credit cards are for. And, let's say that you're at a test site that looks like a good place for survival training; it's ninety-two degrees and not a shred of shade. And, let's say that despite all the magnificent planning, you forgot your hat. Well…that's what your Dogbuddies are for.

My Dogbuddy Pat's Indispensable Stuff

- Crates
- Crate pads or rugs
- Cell phone, charger
- Screens or shade cloth
- Bungee straps
- Fans, extra batteries
- Alligator clips, some magnetic
- First aid kit for dogs and people
- Sunscreen, medicated powder
- Flea spray, Skin-So-Soft
- Wet wipes, paper towels
- Rescue Remedy for calming dogs and humans
- Dog food
- Food pans
- Five-gallon container of water with pour spout
- Snap leads
- Collars
- Slip leads
- Check cord
- Tags and copy of rabies certificate
- Masking tape, adhesive tape
- Grooming supplies
- Grooming table
- Towels
- Flashlights
- Rope/clothesline
- Athletic socks, an extra pair
- Wool socks
- Duck shoes

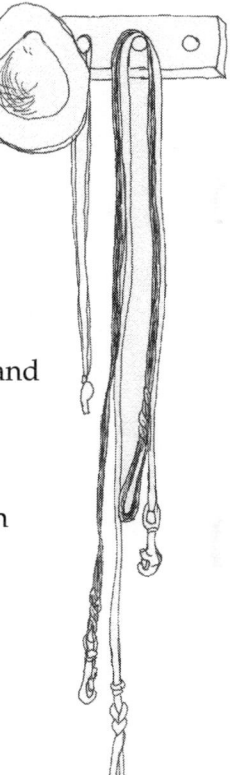

- Knee high rubber boots
- Poncho
- Hats
- Change of clothes
- Fully stocked toolbox
- Maps, GPS
- Thermos
- Picnic supplies, snacks, cooler with cold drinks
- Audio tapes, CDs
- 1qt. oil, automatic transmission fluid, power steering fluid, jumper cables

7

Taking It On the Road

With only a certain amount of well-contained hysteria, you have managed to pack, load up, gas up, bathe the dog, and post the motel telephone number in case of dire need. You have even remembered to leave some food in the refrigerator to keep starvation from the door for those remaining at home. YOU'RE HEADING DOWN THE ROAD.

It's about time for you to show the world just how good you really are. The toughest part of this whole dog game is over. When you are about one hundred miles from home, you might find that you left your food pans behind. Guess what. It really doesn't matter any more. If you're smart enough to have chosen and trained that great dog riding happily behind you, you're probably smart enough to come up with a way to feed him. What is important here is that you are on your way.

Fellow Travelers

Let me take you aside and whisper a certain inalienable truth in your ear. All of your dog friends DO NOT make good traveling companions. This may have already dawned on you. The passenger seat is the place for a Dogbuddy whose company you really enjoy for several hundred miles. My Dogbuddies know that I NEVER run out of conversation EXCEPT first thing in the morning. I'm not mad at anyone, I just need to be very quiet... *very quiet*. They forgive me that. They also marvel at how I have stayed married to a man who leaps out of bed fully awake and VERY cheerful. One of my Dogbuddies really looks forward to a great steak after the show. She really wouldn't be very comfortable with a travel partner who is a devout vegetarian on a mission. It is not necessary or even desirable for all of us to be alike; we just need to be accepting of each others' odd little idiosyncrasies.

You need to do some soul-searching here. You'll be spending more than a little time in the company of the person who is riding with you. You need to know what you can laugh off and what things are really annoying. I have a Dogbuddy who is very punctual. She is miserable when her schedule is ignored. She is one of my best friends, but I drive her CRAZY. I consider ten minutes late to be ON TIME—except for *dog events*. I have always considered tardiness a virtue. I was born two and a half weeks late, and I've been running about that late ever since.

I have finally realized that it is very rude to keep people waiting, and I've really tried to reform, but in the meantime, I am not a good travel companion for my time-conscious friend. She would arrive stressed because we didn't get to the trial five minutes before the fifteen minute grace period she allowed for herself, which was about two hours before the start of her class. I would arrive feeling pushed and nagged and NOT in my usual relaxed mood. We agree on many really important issues, but a travel philosophy is not one of them.

The trait that I most value among my Dogbuddies is a positive attitude. All the way to the hunt test, I want to think of how well things are going to turn out. I want to think about how much fun we are having. When it stops being fun, it's time to stop. It doesn't help to hear a whole litany of potential disaster for the weekend ahead. This is no time for a review of your dog's shortcomings.

It is not reassuring to hear that the judge for your Junior Hunter test despises golden retrievers when you have one smiling at you from his crate. It doesn't help to be reminded of how many times your dog forgot his steadiness lessons and went flying into the water long, long before you sent him. You don't need any lectures on how bad it's going to be if you mess up. This is the time to put those doubts behind you and get on with the job in hand—keeping your dog safe and comfortable and happy. Know that you have done your best for him, and, without question, he will do his best for you.

You can weather all kinds of impending disasters if your Dogbuddies are upbeat. My Dogbuddies haven't been commissioned to keep me amused, but we do seem to find a lot to laugh about. Somehow, the car trouble on the interstate and the terrible food at the only open roadside restaurant don't seem so bad if you're in the right company. John Patrick, the playwright, said, "I guess it has to be exasperating now to be funny later." This must be true, because we have a lot of laughs over incidents that seemed pretty awful at the time.

My Dogbuddy Nancy and I have traveled hundreds of thousands of miles together. She is a veterinarian, so I know that she takes lots of things really seriously, but on dog trips she tends to see the funny side of most situations. We both seem to be on about the same mental clock and the same mindset. We have had a few exhilarating trips where we got to the show, and, miracle of miracles, we found a parking spot, grabbed the dogs, and raced to ringside at the very moment our class was called. Lucky for us, we show a drip-dry breed. I'm not advocating this, but it has happened. We did not spend the rest of the day trying to decide whose fault it was. Was the reason we were rushed because I needed one more cup of coffee at breakfast or because she needed to stop at a supermarket for another pair of pantyhose? Did we care? What we cared about was that we showed our dogs, did our share of winning, and had a good day.

There was only one day when frayed nerves unraveled and we had words. I had a basenji in the ring at the far end of the building. When I got back to my setup, I needed to take a basset hound back to the same ring. If I had understood either the schedule or the alphabet, I might have detected that bassets followed basenjis. Normally, Nancy would have been holding the dog at ringside, but she was showing her dog in obedience. Our usual routine was to buy a can of liver at the beginning of the day, open it, drain it, and have it ready to use. Generally, whichever of us had a few minutes would do this. I put Mac's lead on. NO LIVER! Now, Mac was a very nice, sound basset and very easygoing. You couldn't show him without bait because, without it, he had NO WRINKLES. Do NOT plan to win with a basset with no wrinkles. As I fought my way back to the ring, I passed Nancy. I shouted, "Where the heck is the liver?" Responding to my somewhat hostile tone, she replied, "Well, WHO put ME in charge of liver?" I borrowed some bait at ringside and showed the dog, who was totally unaware of the high drama. Actually, he was totally unaware of most things. By the time we returned to the setup, it had occurred to both of us how really hilarious our exchange had been.

To this day, if anyone around us gets out of line and becomes just a little too officious, one or the other of us will say, "Well, WHO put HER in charge of liver?" It's still good for a laugh.

The point being? Use great care in choosing your fellow travelers. They'll be with you for the thrill of victory but also for the agony of defeat. It goes without saying that they'll be with you when you are stressed, tired, disappointed, and plain grouchy. Don't let the minor annoyances get in the way of a good time or a good friendship. Remember, your real Dogbuddies can overlook most things, and what they cannot overlook, they're certain to forgive.

Keeping Up Your Strength

It doesn't matter whether your trip is across town to the local fairgrounds or across the country to a national specialty. (For the uninitiated, a specialty is a show and its related dog events, limited to a specific breed.) Regardless, you have to have an ice chest filled with everyone's favorite snacks, cold drinks, and bottled water. You need that water to stay hydrated. Besides, you will look very upscale later when you are walking around with your enormously expensive bottle of San Peregrino. No one needs to know that you refilled it from the kitchen sink.

It's a good idea to bring sandwich makings in case you're driving through an area that, by some remote chance, is without a McDonald's in sight. You were careful enough to bring plenty of food for the dogs, the least you can do is to make sure you remembered the can of cashews for yourself.

If you are like me, you take the first driving shift. I can drive for hours in the morning, but I like to stop, stretch my legs and have lunch somewhere that I can sit down. Lunch usually makes me feel sleepy, so it is someone else's turn while I have rest hour. There is always one of your Dogbuddies who is glad to have you start out while they are getting their bearings. My Dogbuddies and I like to stop someplace that looks as though maybe the food is edible. When all else fails, we can stop at a fast food place, but often we can find a place that doesn't take forever and the food is better.

Riding Shotgun

When it is not your turn to drive, you have major tasks other than nap taking. First and foremost, you are the navigator. With modern technology, you have at your fingertips everything you need to get from Point A to Point B. It should be clearly understood, however, if you do instruct the driver to make a left turn that ultimately leads you onto the parade grounds at the Air Force Academy, IT IS NOBODY'S FAULT and eventually you will get yourselves to the agility event.

It is your sworn responsibility to open soft drinks for the driver and spread the cheese on the crackers. It helps if you can maintain a conversation, but sometimes a companionable grunt every now and then will do.

You are the lookout for the Holiday Inn, and you assist in selecting the right exits. If, inadvertently, the driver makes a wrong turn, it is your holy obligation to say, "That's okay, we can double back. We have plenty of time." No whining. No complaining. It is considered to be in extremely poor taste to shout, "How could you have missed that turn?"

Maps and Compasses

When I first started traveling to dog events, I would use a map that they gave me at the gas station. This was probably a place where they actually pumped my gas and cleaned my windshield. Well, those days are dead and gone forever. Here in the twenty-first century, we have Map Blast or other related websites where you can enter the address of your destination and VOILA!!, you can print out a map that will direct you there.

OR you can rely on…

The Directions in Your Premium List

Generally, these directions are reasonably clear and, if followed correctly, will get you there. Directions always make sense when you know exactly where you are going. However, when you are a child in the wilderness, they can be very confusing. They usually have been prepared in good faith. The purpose in publishing them was to get you to the event. These directions are generally free of errors and will achieve the goal. Be forewarned, however, that in certain circumstances I have felt that they were totally undecipherable, and it crossed my mind that they were prepared by the competition.

Cell Phones

When someone came up with wireless communications, they must have realized that they had committed an act of mercy. No one single device has saved me from more potential disasters. Cell phones are just plain comforting. No matter how self-sufficient you think you are, you must NEVER venture more than a mile from home without yours. You can safely summon help in an emergency. Assistance from your auto club might take a while to turn up, but it DOES turn up. Even when there is no impending disaster, a cell phone comes in really handy when you need to bear tidings of joy for your magnificent group placement/long sought after Utility title/perfect run.

GPS

In my recent travels, I have made use of a Global Positioning System (GPS). This device is linked to a constellation of satellites for the express purpose of telling you where in the world you are. The first time I took it with me, I was overwhelmed with its complexity and frustrated because I couldn't figure out how to use it. My husband said, with just a touch of condescension, "Now look, you're an intelligent woman. You don't need to be a rocket scientist to understand this." Easy for him to say; he is one. Nevertheless, I learned the fundamentals and took the thing with me.

The GPS will get you there as the crow flies. If by chance you are not traveling by crow, you will soon learn that the GPS indicates the correct direction of your destination and the shortest path. It does not take into consideration fences, bodies of water, and other obstacles. Therefore, it needs to be used in conjunction with your map and printed directions.

My Dogbuddy Gillian and I discovered this on the way to a field site in Colorado. GPS in hand, we journeyed over hill and dale, always in the right direction, if not on the fastest route. Ultimately, we found ourselves within an eighth of a mile of the site in the MIDDLE OF A FEED LOT. We had to resort to finding the field headquarters the old fashioned way. We ASKED.

Having said all that, the GPS is a useful device. If the waypoints are put in accurately and you make use of other navigational aids, it can really keep you from going twenty miles in the wrong direction.

Caravanning

Dog people tend to travel in groups. Usually we meet at some predetermined central location and proceed to the event in what resembles a rather loosely organized convoy. It begins to look a little like follow the leader. We take too many dogs collectively to travel in the same vehicle, but we like the idea of traveling together. I'm not always in love with gadgets, but we all have our favorites. Mine is a two-way radio. It's a pretty unsophisticated model—not too many whistles and bells—but it has a range of a mile or so and lets me communicate with the van ahead of me. We used to signal and wave and shout at each other at the traffic lights. We ran the risk of letting total strangers in the next lane believe that we wanted to meet them at the Cracker Barrel. Not a good idea. Two-way radios are less expensive than cell phones, have no monthly fees or hookup charges, and, at fairly close range, they'll keep you in touch.

Caravanning keeps the group together, avoids waits for the stragglers, and either none of us are lost, or we all get lost.

The Friendly Skies

Contrary to popular belief, all dog events are not within driving distance. Sometimes the combination of too many miles and too little time really works against you. Consider airline travel. Come on, just think about it. You will hear horror stories of dogs missing for hours or arriving in poor condition. Sure, there have been nervous dogs who suffered from post-traumatic syndrome. But, here's the good news. Every year thousands of dogs are flown safely and hop out of their crates perfectly happy, none the worse for wear.

My dogs are Frequent Flyers, so I can help you out here. First of all, your dog shouldn't be going ANYWHERE unless he is healthy. When he flies, he has his health certificate to prove his well being. This is not your regular vaccination record but a special document designed for travel. You add this little item to your pre-travel agenda just in case you didn't have enough things to worry about. Or maybe you hadn't spent quite enough money. He will fly within two weeks of the time he was examined and found to be perfect in every way. Well, of course you think he's perfect, but in this case it's important for your vet to think so, too. Your airborne Dogbuddies will tell you that the ticket agents almost never ask to see it, but I can promise you that the first time you show up WITHOUT a health certificate, you will be asked for it. If you can't produce it, your dog will NOT be on the plane. DO NOT SHOW UP AT THE AIRPORT

WITHOUT YOUR CERTIFICATE. I REPEAT…well, never mind, you get the point.

Here's the great advantage of early crate training. The crate is your dog's home away from home—same house, different sky. Most airlines require your presence at the ticket counter one and one-half to two hours before your flight. Good thinking. If you give the airlines plenty of time, they can get you and the dog safely boarded on the same flight. Fill a small stainless bucket with ice, and clip it to the door of the crate. By now, your dog is in his crate, complete with identification tags on his collar. Not to take any chances, he is microchipped. You present yourself at the ticket counter. After long minutes of what appears to be soul searching, the computer will somehow, quite magically, produce your boarding pass.

After a small eternity, you will have a form to fill out to identify the crate. I put my dog's call name on it. He appreciates it when the baggage carriers are on a first name basis with him. I tell them, of course, that he prefers to be called Alexander and not Al.

I like for my dog to stay with me as long as possible before heading down to the gate. Before leaving him, I check one more time to make sure that all those little bolts on his airline crate are tight. (Okay, so it sounds a little obsessive, but I have this reoccurring dream about Alexander cleverly slipping out of his crate and frantically searching the airport for me—or lunch.) He gets a brisk, calm good-bye. No sad farewells. Keep this upbeat, and he'll feel better for it.

Help the airline personnel realize how much you like this dog. You probably are concerned, so go ahead and act like it. I ask EVERYONE in airline uniforms if they would tell me when my dog has been loaded onto the aircraft. I ask the ticket agent, I ask each and every flight attendant, as I am boarding, if they will tell me the moment that my dog is safely on the plane. I sound a little repetitive, but they get the message that I am WORRIED. Generally, three different people come to tell me that my dog is on the plane. They all have dogs, too, and even if they think I'm a little neurotic, they understand.

I was flying to Arizona. I was scrunched into my seat. Some business major must have decided that knee room was something that was only to be accorded to First Class legs. From the window, I had seen Alexander's crate being carefully lifted aboard. I knew that we were both going to the same place, so I settled down to a good mystery, my current form of airplane literature.

After take-off, the captain's voice, deep and reassuring as captains are supposed to sound, was heard throughout the aircraft. "This is Captain Eckerly. We are at a cruising altitude of thirty-seven thousand feet. We should be arriving in Phoenix at 1:37 Mountain Standard Time after a flying time of two hours and thirty-two minutes. With clear skies in Phoenix, we should be looking forward to a sunny seventy-six degrees. I hope you are having a pleasant flight...and to the passenger who is traveling with her dog, Alexander is riding happily in his compartment, which is climate controlled at sixty-eight degrees. He is probably just a little more comfortable than you are. Have a good trip." I did. It's nice to have Dogbuddies in high places.

Home Away From Home

Premium lists contain, among all their other pearls of wisdom, a list of hotels and motels that accept dogs. They may not be the most luxurious, but they are normally clean, safe, and adequate. Make your reservations early. If not, some of our Type A brethren will have taken all the rooms, and you'll find yourself at someplace whose only name is MOTEL. I've stayed in a few of those, and it seemed to me that some of the other guests either required very little sleep or they were on a very tight schedule. Guarantee your stay on a credit card to secure your room for a late arrival. WHY do I think you might need that?

But Will They Love You Tomorrow?

I'm not going to suggest that you take the same care of your motel room as you do your home. No. I'm going to suggest that you take ten times better care. If we "dog people" mess up, literally and figuratively, too many more times, THERE WILL BE NO ROOM AT THE INN.

Clubs offering events for the rest of us to exhibit our dogs contact nearby hotels and motels to see if they accept dogs. If they do, they are published in the premium list. From that moment on, they are at our mercy. Can you believe it? Sometimes they actually give us lower rates. You have to wonder why. Rooms have been trashed. One hotel set up a bath area out back complete with stacks of fresh towels exclusively for the dogs, and still a few were bathed in the bathrooms. Really, we can do better than this.

Remember that old adage about "leaving a place better than you found it"? This would be an outstanding time to practice it. Before my dog's paws ever touch the carpet of my room, I make sure that it is ready for him. I find the right corner for his crate and place it on a waterproof sheet. I put his pans on the tile in the bathroom. I'm not as brave as some of my fellow wayfarers. I bring my dog into my room on lead and let him relax in his crate. He will be quiet, as I would not enjoy being evicted. He has been taught to stay off the furniture and has been house trained since he was eight weeks old, but this is no time to take chances. Generally, I don't obsess over things, but I want to be invited back; and I want all of you there, too.

Som hotels develop rules for guests with dogs. They must have reasons for posting them. It's a good idea to follow them. Take a look at the "Paw Laws" handed out by the headquarters hotel for a national speciality. My dogbuddies took them seriously and obviously the hotel did.

"Paw Laws"

- Only two (2) LARGE dogs or four (4) small dogs are allowed per room.
- Dogs must be crated when you are not in the room.
- When you have your dog(s) out of the room, they must be kept under control and have a collar and leash on.
- "Accidents" happen—please call the Front Desk to let us know so that we may clean the spot quickly.
- Organizers of the event will provide each guest with a door sign that alerts people that there is a dog in the guest room.
- Housekeeping will not enter any room where the dog is not crated—if you would like to have your room cleaned, please crate your dog.
- All grooming must be done outside in the specified grooming areas or at the show site.
- The bathtubs and sinks may not be used to bathe your dogs, as this clogs the drains. Housekeeping will check the drains on a daily basis and there will be an additional fee of $35 for repairs.
- Do not allow the dogs on the furniture unless you have covered the furnitute with a sheet.
- Hotel linens and towels may not be used to bathe your dog and these items may not be removed from the hotel.
- Do not use the ice buckets for dog food or water.
- Walking areas will be clearly posted—trash cans and "Pooper Scoopers" will be available in these areas.
- Excessive barking or howling in the hotel guest room or parking lot will be asked to check-out of the Hotel.
- Dogs may not be taken into the restaurant or lounge areas.
- Please remember that not everyone loves your dogs as much as you do and may be frightened of them. Please keep them on a short leash when walking through the hotel and parking lot.

Any abuse of the above "paw laws" will be noted and reported to the event organizer.

8

Staying on Top of Your Game

Nothing can ruin your day as fast as a sick dog.

You're heading to the show. You're singing along with Garth. All's right with the world. Just then, from the dark recesses of your dog's crate, you hear an odd sound. All of your Dog-buddies recognize it instantly. A little cough, then a louder retching noise, and then full-blown heaving from the depth of your dog's stomach. You may not be off to a good start.

Usually these things have a very ordinary beginning. My Dog-buddy Diney was trying hard to be a really good dog mom. Before loading her dog into the van, she gave her the chance to stretch her legs. This Chesapeake did the only sensible thing. She took full advantage of her freedom. It was one of those hot mornings, temperature already in the eighties, with a relative humidity of ninety-seven percent. She made the rounds of the front yard at breakneck speed and then jumped enthusiastically into her crate. Taking the edge off her thirst, she drank a bucket of water—Chessie fashion—from the bottom first, and off they went. You can probably figure out the rest of the story. Ten minutes down the road an ominous sound was heard throughout the land. The Chessie lost the bucket of water, all of her breakfast, and something that was once a good crop of St. Augustine grass.

Wasn't it thoughtful of Diney's dog to choose to cough up her cookies on the way to a *local* show site? At least, they didn't have to pull over on I-75 to deal with the mess. Taking care of business first, Diney checked the dog to make sure that the problem was nothing more than gulped water. The dog seemed to be her normal self, just a little sheepish, and she swallowed her Pepto Bismol tablet without complaint. (You don't want to use the liquid form unless you think that pink, chalky stuff enhances your dog's appearance.) Diney, trying to be her normal self, went about the business of restoring some semblance of order to her van.

Cleaning the crate of a sick dog is not one of life's more pleasant experiences. Someone holds the dog who, by this time, feels fine and is somewhat amused. Have you ever noticed that dog crates become longer and skinnier when you are trying to clean them with nothing but some paper towels and your bare hands? Diney, armed with disinfectant, returned the crate to its former, clean condition.

Hands washed, a damp cloth run over the dog, and the two walked into the ring, both of them totally unruffled. Now, that has to be an acquired skill—crawl into a nasty dog crate and fifteen minutes later walk into a showring calm, cool, collected, and your makeup still intact. This can happen; it did.

We have some priorities here. Rule 1) THE DOG'S HEALTH COMES FIRST. After that you can worry about all the other problems. NOTHING takes precedence over Rule 1. Rule 2) RULE 1 NEVER CHANGES.

You might spend ten exciting minutes exhibiting a dog after six months of planning, training, and preparation. That's okay. I can honestly say that the time I spend getting my dog ready and keeping him that way is the best part of the whole thing. Your dog has no choice other than to trust his health and welfare to you. Get this part right, and the rest should come easy.

Your Dogbuddies would hate to worry you about all the things that can go wrong. On the other hand, it's a good idea always to be ready for anything. Gather 'round, and let me tell you the story of the show season that went wrong. Bad things happen in threes. How do I know that? Because my Dogbuddy Pat told me so, and she's usually right about things. First, there was the tornado in Macon that brought the show to a complete halt. A few weeks later, the field next to my ring caught on fire, and we continued with the group judging while the fire department put out the fire. The show must go on. Finally, there was the flood in Pensacola. When the indoor rings were submerged, the show was called off. I began to think there was a message for me in all of this.

Being a typical dog person, I realized that if you go to enough dog events, some pretty odd things will happen. You may as well be ready for them. When they can affect your dog's health and well being, you can use all the help you can get.

The Doctor Is In

All veterinarians have their diplomas and certifications, tastefully framed, of course, and prominently displayed on the walls of their clinic. It comes as no great surprise to you that your vet went to an accredited veterinary school and was successfully graduated. If you had any doubts about that, you wouldn't be there in the first place. Basics out of the way, what is really important in the great vet search?

Your Dogbuddies are all looking for James Herriot, the charming and lovable hero of *All Creatures Great and Small*. We need someone with leading edge medical knowledge, great diagnostic skills, (your dog can't tell him where it hurts) combined with old-fashioned dog-sense. I know that the vet probably wouldn't have made this career choice if he or she didn't like animals, but I watch carefully to see how he or she treats mine. It may be just a word or a touch, but I can tell. I took Will in one day for a blood test. It took a minute to draw the blood, and when it was done, my veterinarian, Dr. John Miller, laid his hand gently on Will's shoulder and very quietly said, "You're a brave dog." He had me forever.

You need to be able to talk to your vet, and he needs to be able to listen. He needs to be able to understand your objectives. It's two weeks before the show. You're trying to treat a small hot spot on your keeshond's muzzle, judge's side, of course. You need a vet who understands that you might not want the entire left side of the dog's head shaved. And one more thing: If your dog has a problem that requires a specialist, you want a veterinarian who has enough confidence to make a referral without feeling threatened.

If you've found all this in one human, you're on the right track. Oh, and one more thing...

Cleanliness Is Next to Godliness

I've decided that the mainstay of the dog fancy is bleach. My Dogbuddies and I have used millions of gallons of the stuff. I finish my morning cleaning chores, shower, and dress. I'm ready to go. I'm trying to do an impression of a normal, every day non-dog person. But what is that lingering fragrance? Chanel? Christian Dior? No, it's Clorox—plain old-fashioned bleach. I am haunted by the thought of running out of it. I dilute it and scrub kennels. I clean crates with it. It's in the washer along with the dog rugs. You can't escape the smell of it. I don't even mind the smell of it. As a matter of fact, I feel pretty smug about it. My Dogbuddies come early to train and know I've been cleaning. I use some antibacterial stuff, too, but I just can't get away from Clorox.

That beautiful floating Irish setter whose coat you admire is the proof of hours of care. It all started with one concept. Cleanliness. You're not going to find a substitute for it. It starts with clean bedding and clean food pans and water dishes. There was a time that you stumbled into the kitchen in the morning, poured coffee, and slowly opened your eyes. Now, you air dogs, measure out food, give fresh water, and check eyes and ears for problems. Okay, you're ready for coffee.

Cleaning up after your dogs and keeping them clean is a job you can count on. You will never become obsolete. That's the good news.

Conditioning

Haven't you seen those nostalgic stories of Olympic athletes in their hometowns? Sure, sometimes they are having pizza with the family, but mainly you see them running or skiing or falling on the ice and trying again. What you do not see is the athlete, human or otherwise, lying around the house from Monday to Friday and then competing in top form on the weekend. You wouldn't see him or her winning either.

Every dog sport, from conformation to fly ball, requires dogs to be in condition. Breed standards call for dogs in "hard, working condition." Take agility or field or lure coursing—they all demand stamina. Obedience jumping exercises require a strong agile body. Well, don't we all want that?

So it stands to reason that all dogs involved in dog sports need to be in condition. Okay, you can take this to the bank. I will not be running my dog five miles a day to get him in shape. Some of my Dogbuddies do. My dogs go for walks where they can maintain an easy trot for a half hour or so and find interesting things to think about. That's much more my style.

It only makes sense to get into shape gradually—a little work every day. Months when your dog's exercise consists mainly of walking over to his food pan, with occasional sessions of hard exercise, is not going to do it. I like retrieving. It doesn't matter if it's a training dummy or a favorite ball. It could be a retrieve where he flies up a hill, or it could be out of the water. My job is to throw—not too tough—and theirs is to fetch, which is the joy of their lives. I may get pond water shaken all over me, but at least I'm not hot and sweaty.

Some of my Dogbuddies have dog exercisers, sort of a canine treadmill. If you have no good way to get your dogs out or you can't bear the thought of a walk, that might be the answer. I've always thought, though, that it would bore the dogs to death. It would also give them more time to plot against me—something I don't actually need.

Christine Zink, DVM, PhD, is a foremost authority on the dog as an athlete. Catch one of her seminars. There are some excellent materials written for people with canine athletes. Wait for a tropical depression or some other kind of sustained weather pattern, and settle down and read them.

Things That Itch

Even dogs that are genetically programmed to have good coats can be sabotaged by parasites. You've got to do something. My suggestion is all-out warfare. If you can't get rid of these pests with ordinary measures, see a professional. You can use a preventative product for fleas and ticks. Read the label carefully; read all of it before putting even one drop on your dog or yard. Chemicals used improperly can be *fatal*. There's a reason for putting those warnings on the package.

You may as well forget keeping your dog's coat in good condition if these little varmints bother him. If his skin is in poor condition, his coat is bound to follow. Persistent scratching damages a coat, and chewing absolutely destroys it. It's a funny thing about dog show judges. They notice those bare places where furnishings were supposed to be.

As if that isn't bad enough, what do you suppose happens in obedience? First your dog is sitting quietly on a Long Sit. He's qualifying. All he needs to do here is SIT STILL, but no. First there is a little scratch just behind the ear. That leads to a bout of frantic scratching. Next, your beloved dog shakes himself off and STANDS, and then he sniffs the Australian terrier next to him. That's the end of your CD for that day. The terrier gets to try again, but her owner tells you, in no uncertain terms, that your dog made her dog break. "After that, she was too upset to be able to sit even for a second, much less a minute. She probably would have had First Place." Not good. Chances are, this fellow exhibitor will never become one of your Dogbuddies.

Toenails

One of the more terrifying tasks you will have to perform is toenail trimming. Before you tell me that you'll get the vet to do it, I'm going to explain why it is best done at home. A veterinary clinic can be something less than pleasant for young, impressionable dogs. It doesn't look like anyplace they've seen before. Bigger dogs menace them as you're trying to get through the door, and then there is that odd, hospital smell. Your puppy thinks that this is a very exciting place if he's an outgoing type or a frightening place if he isn't. Veterinary technicians, who are the folks who normally do the toenail trimming, don't have tons of time to gently introduce your pup to what can be a fairly simple procedure. If your puppy is wiggling (and most are), he will be firmly restrained. He won't like it and will struggle. Pretty soon everyone is struggling, and the quick (that pink vein that runs down the inside of the toenail) is nicked. It hurts, and the puppy's fondness for toenail trimming is now a thing of the past.

Here's my technique. It's a two-person job. First, find a quiet place for you and your pup and your Dogbuddy to sit. Have ready your toenail trimmers and some moistened cotton swabs and a styptic powder, such as Kwik Stop (a powder coagulant), just in case. Have your helper hold a REALLY good soft treat and let the puppy nibble it. At the same time, your helper will hold the place behind the puppy's elbow securely to allow the paw to relax. When the puppy is engrossed in licking his treat, you can snip off the very end of the toenail—not more than a sixteenth of an inch. If the toenails are white, it is easy to see where the quick begins. If they are black, use great caution, and trim again in a few days, just a little at a time.

Have a dress rehearsal. Tap each toenail gently and give a treat. Tell your puppy what an absolute prince he is and let it go for the day. The next day you can trim for real. What if, horror of horrors, you nick the quick? In dog parlance this is called "quicking." Obviously, it's happened before, and the dog survived. Simply apply the cotton swab dipped in Kwik Stop firmly to the end of the toenail. In a few seconds, the bleeding will stop, and your house will not look like a scene from *Friday the 13th*.

I prefer the clippers that work like scissors rather than the guillotine type. The guillotine clippers tend to crush the nail, and I think it makes the process a little more uncomfortable. Many of my Dogbuddies like them better, so perhaps it is what you become accustomed to. You can trim all the nails quickly in one sitting or a few nails at a time. One poodle breeder I knew went through her whole kennel and trimmed one nail on each dog per day. It was done quickly and the dog got a treat. One of them would hold up his paw whenever he saw her. He thought the trick was: Step 1) Hold up paw; Step 2) Trim toenail; Step 3) Get a cookie.

Some of my Dogbuddies use a grinder instead of clippers. A Dremel tool can be used to smooth off the nail.

If this whole discussion leaves you faintly nauseated, find a Dogbuddy to help you. Let's say you're an artist at trimming ears. Maybe you have a Dogbuddy who is great at nail trimming but hates to do ears. It's a perfect match.

You might find that trimming toenails is easier than it sounds. Be brave. Give it a try. We are not talking about brain surgery here.

Teeth

I'm of the hard biscuits and dry kibble persuasion when it comes to keeping my dog's teeth clean. I do have their teeth and gums checked every time we see the vet. Apparently that combination works, because my dogs have avoided any dental problems. Tarter buildup, the leading cause of gum disease, seems to be affected by genetics, so maybe I just got lucky. If there is odor, chances are there is a buildup of tarter. Off to the veterinarian's to get it removed. You want to keep those smiles bright, don't you?

Short Course in First Aid

This is NOT a detailed course in canine first aid. Take a course in canine first aid. If you can't find one, organize one. Get a class or club to help sponsor it. Think of the community service you'll be rendering. Ask your vet if he or she would teach it for you or knows someone who would. In this section, I'll give you the bare essentials and trust you to go forth and seek out knowledge.

Your dog counts on you to be observant. You know when something is NOT right. If any one of my dogs misses a meal, I know I'm in trouble. They are all very eager eaters, and when they leave food in their pans, I start looking for a problem. If your dog is known for his pickiness, ignore that last thought. But there might be some other symptom that is out of character for your dog, and you will recognize it with the acuity of a mother lioness.

The Temperature's Rising

Your dog, who is usually full of energy, doesn't want to move. He ignores breakfast. He feels warm to the touch. I'd get out the thermometer. Your dog's normal temperature, taken rectally, is between 101 and 102 degrees. If it is *more than 105 degrees* or *less than 100 degrees*, go directly to the vet. This is no time for home health measures.

Poisoning

If you even think that your dog has swallowed something poisonous, call the *Poison Information Center*. The number should be listed inside the front cover of your telephone book. Knowing how careful you are, you have already looked it up and posted it with any other emergency numbers. These poison centers are generally affiliated with the American Association of Poison Control Centers. If your dog was kind enough to bring you the container, tell the listener the active ingredients and keep the container. Follow the recommendations for treatment. Again, head for the vet immediately.

Too Much Heat

Any dog sport can be a golden opportunity for a problem with heat. Outdoor rings, parking areas at hunt tests, an agility run at noon. Any of these delights have the potential for your dog to become overheated. At best, he is a little hot and panting, and, at worst, he has fully developed heatstroke. That's not a happy thought.

My Dogbuddies always look for a shady place to park. You have to get there early, because all the good spots go fast. We have battery driven fans directed at our dogs to keep the air circulating. We have reflective blankets to keep the sun off. We carry plenty of water and Kwik-Kold, an instant ice pack. You'll have to really watch for signs of overheating. If your dog seems a little too warm, wetting his belly helps. If he has rapid, heavy panting and raspy breathing, you'll want to get his body temperature down and fast. If there is a pond handy, take him in, or find a hose and get him thoroughly soaked. Wrap ice in a towel, and put it on his belly and at the base of his skull. If he can drink, give him small sips of ice water. In serious cases, the dog will actually collapse. Find a vet.

Eyes and Ears

As part of your morning rounds you will notice any eye or ear problems. These things are easier to clear up when they are first noticed. Some dogs never seem to have irritated eyes or ears, and with others it's a constant battle.

Look for any discharge or inflammation. Watch for redness or any odor in the ear. These are not good signs.

Keep handy some saline solution for eyes. Don't bother with the ones designed for humans. Those little containers will be used up in the dog's eye in one squirt. When the dog is running in the field, he can pick up weed seeds in his eyes. A good flush with an eyewash should take care of them. Or you may have to nudge them out with a folded tissue…gently.

Ear problems can get out of hand. On Monday, the dog's ear looks a little pink, and the next day it is hot and red and there is nasty brown gunk in it. If your dog is planning on having a chronic problem, you need to understand it and get professional help. Once fixed, keep it under control with a drying agent such as vinegar and water—a fifty/fifty solution—on a weekly basis. And did I mention vigilance? That head shaking means something.

Sick as a Dog

Reading this is like taking a psych course. You start thinking of symptoms, and you think you are every kind of crazy there is. Now, wait, you know that your dog can't have all of these maladies, but is he holding his head funny? Does he have a scratch, a bump? If you're home, you can try the home cure method for everything except dire emergencies. If, after twenty-four hours you're still not sure, load him up, and drive to the vet.

Now, let's say your medical emergency strikes while you are at a hunt test in the middle of what appears to be NOWHERE. Calmly give First Aid; that's why you bothered to learn about it. Send someone to the test committee to find the location of the nearest vet or emergency clinic. Get someone to take you there.

The good part of having a sick or hurt dog at a dog event is that—here it comes—there are dog people there. Lots of them will know what to do, and all of them will care. Who knows, some of your best Dogbuddies could be veterinarians.

Dogbuddies First Aid Kit

- Emergency numbers
- Animal Poison Control Hotline
- Rectal thermometer
- Water based lubricating jelly
- Sterile gloves
- Instant ice pack
- 4-inch gauze pads
- 1- or 2-inch vet wrap
- Blunt-tipped scissors
- Kwik Stop styptic powder
- Soft muzzle
- Alcohol swabs
- Hydrogen peroxide
- Eye wash
- Ear cleaner
- Antibiotic ointment
- Hydrocortisone
- Cotton balls
- Cotton swabs
- Kwik-Kold ice packs
- Pepto Bismol tablets

9

Food, Glorious Food

In your self-appointed role as your dog's protector, you have spent hours researching canine nutrition. It's something you thought about long before the puppy was even a twinkle in his sire's eye. Natural food? Name brands? Treats? Raw meat? Vegetables? At first glance, it may seem that everything that goes in one end comes out the other, but not quite. Mysterious things happen to food en route to the pooper scooper.

What's for Dinner?

Some dogs will eat anything that doesn't walk away. They aren't picky and seem to prosper on any fairly nourishing dog food. Most of mine thought that eating was on about the same level as retrieving and just a little better than sex. (We breed very sparingly here, so maybe they didn't have too much experience.) Most of my dogs finish off their suppers before I can get all the water bowls filled. If one of them doesn't eat every speck, I check to see if he or she is sick.

You don't have to convince me that you want to feed the very best to your dog. I know that your kids are eating chicken fingers and French fries three times a week, and you worry if the minerals in your designer dog food are not chelated. You're not exactly sure what that is, but you know that you're supposed to look for it. You read the nutritional analysis on the back of the package as though it was the topic of your doctoral thesis. That's good.

Good nutrition translates itself into healthy dogs. We're talking about the kind of good health that makes its appearance in a beautiful coat, bright eyes, and strong bones. Your Saint might not show the same energy that my Dogbuddy's Jack Russell does, but they are both definitely alert and happy.

Dog Foods

Dog food companies go to a lot of expense to lure you into purchasing their product. They have scores of marketing people who stay up nights thinking up warm, fuzzy ways of presenting their product. You watch an ad on TV and get a lump in your throat. After you've recovered your composure, you grab the keys and race out to buy a bag of something that is no better for your four-footed friend than the stuff on your shelf. I ask you, isn't there a better way to go about this?

Your Breeder

Most purebred puppies come with whole sets of instructions: how to feed, what to feed, and how much. Breeders have been raising and feeding your dogs for a while. They will recommend a food and tell you how much to feed. They usually take it as one of their sworn duties. By all means, take their advice, and feed the diet your puppy knows best. This doesn't mean that you can never change products, but the recommended food is a good place to start.

Your Vet

Veterinarians are in the business of keeping your dog healthy. They are not going to recommend food that is not good for your dog. Many veterinarians sell dog food products and will recommend them. In many clinics, there is someone who has really made him or herself familiar with the various products. It's okay to ask why he or she likes a certain food.

My veterinarian, who knows what he is talking about, advocates keeping a puppy a little thin. We're not talking about skinny puppies, simply puppies who don't put on too much weight too fast. If you ever went to Weight Watchers, your fearless leader would have told you that excess weight does you no good at all. It's hard on your joints and bad for your heart. It follows, then, that the same thing is true of your dog. Besides, he is a canine athlete. Most of the people standing on the podiums at the Olympics with those medals around their necks are not overweight. They have to be in great shape. Maybe it's too soon for us to expect to see agility at the Olympics, but why not? After all, there are equestrian events—why not dogs? In the meantime, we'll keep ourselves busy getting our dogs ready to win.

Fellow Exhibitors

You're watching a dog streaking around an agility course. He doesn't look as though he's had a down day in his whole life. He's in great shape. He looks beautiful. What do they feed that dog? Everyone in dogs has his or her favorite dog food products. Your Dogbuddies can give you the nutritional analysis and discuss the ingredients. Dog people love to talk about their dogs. Ask a simple question, and you will receive an avalanche of information.

Forthcoming is a basic truth: The same dog food may not be right for every dog. It becomes obvious when you notice that five different dogs eat five different dog foods, and they all thrive.

Kibble Over Canned

My Dogbuddy Joan brushes her dogs' teeth daily. I wish I was that dedicated. My less fortunate dogs eat a diet of high quality dog food kibble and get hard biscuits to keep their teeth and gums healthy. It's worked so far, but I wonder if they'd be happier over at Joan's house, curled up next to her and having their teeth brushed with something that tastes like liverwurst.

A good kibble provides all those nice little nutrients and has the recommended balance of protein, fat, and fiber. It's my opinion that canned food is about eighty percent water. It adds flavor but not much more. I like to think the manufacturers of a good quality food have done their research and applied it to their product without too many cost-saving compromises. When it says "chicken meal," I want it to mean chicken meal and not something they swept off the floor. I'm a sucker for a product that contains some brown rice and whole wheat. I don't know if dogs need these things, but they sound so HEALTHY.

You may have to try a few, but you will find a kibble that your dog likes. Most of my Dogbuddies feed it dry. I have moistened it with chicken broth to encourage a dog to eat, but the product I feed now is palatable, and it doesn't stay in their food pans long. It may take a few tries before you find a food that gives you that good overall condition. With a little luck, the dog will eat it.

Designer Dog Foods

You can tell if you are feeding a "Designer Dog Food" if it costs more than the food at the grocery store. Is it better? Maybe. Most of the "high end" dog foods are more concentrated. It's Rice Krispies vs. Grapenuts Flakes. Although the product costs more, you feed less. And the payoff is that there is less stool to clean up, and it's not as yucky. Now, that's a marketing approach I can understand.

I worry about cancer in dogs, so I look for a product that is preserved naturally and avoids a lot of chemicals. I don't like the stuff that has number two red dye in it. That red food dye is for our benefit, not the dog's. Do those dog food manufacturers really think that our dogs look at their biscuit and think, "Wow! That must be my own little lamb chop." I'm not sure how your dog feels about food. Alexander thinks that if it smells remotely like food, he can swallow it before it has spent much time with his taste buds. I don't think that he is giving his biscuits a critique to see how closely they resemble a T-bone steak. Let me tell you, if it was a T-bone steak, he'd know it.

Check the date on the package to make sure the product is fresh. When that rancid smell is coming from the food you just opened, TAKE IT BACK; it's not fresh. Trust your nose. If the kibble is clumped together, it probably got wet. TAKE IT BACK. If the food is dry on top and oily on the bottom, something went wrong with quality control. TAKE IT BACK. We humans eat a variety of foods. The chocolate milkshakes are balanced by the grilled chicken. If we are drinking a nutritionally bereft Coke, it is not our only source of nourishment. Our dogs, however, eat the same food every day, twice a day, sometimes for a lifetime. It better be good.

The high-end products have one other advantage. You will be offered a variety of formulas from which to select. You could have the choice of two slightly different kibbles for puppies, one for very young pups or small breeds, another for larger breeds. There is light food, food for the high activity dog who requires a higher caloric intake, food for the older dog, and food for the dog with allergies. Whatever it is that you think your dog needs, there will be some product that will provide it. Read the nutritional information carefully. Somewhere out there some dog food company has your dog in mind.

Home Cookin'

I have Dogbuddies who are slaving over a hot stove. They actually cook all of their dogs' food. They prefer a holistic approach to feeding and don't want to worry about chicken feathers winding up in the dog food. They have done their homework and are careful to make sure the dogs are getting the right balance of nutrients. They understand how to balance the ingredients so that the food contains all of the essential nutrients. They have done a study of the vitamin and mineral requirements for their dogs. They've read books and attended seminars on nutrition. For me to get it right, I'd have to take a university level course.

Can it be done? Sure, and if you enjoy cooking for your dogs and have done the research, why not?

Preparing dog food comes pretty far down on my own list. Besides, it would be bad to cook for the dogs and then ask my husband to take me out to dinner. The only times I cook for my dogs are when they are sick or old. Then, I can cook chicken and rice along with the best of them. Still, those noble chef dog people should receive special awards or, at the very least, appear with Martha Stewart.

Treats

Having said that, you should know that we do bake for the dogs at my training school. I need a soft treat for training and don't like the commercial ones, soooo I started baking something that I fondly call Pâté Cakes. They look like brownies but are made of liver. Pretty funny. My Dogbuddy Donna, who is the other half of the Baking Committee, claims that it is not the Pâté baking that is hard. It is the cleaning up. If the batter is not washed off the utensils instantly, it hardens into something that closely resembles tile grout. I've never baked an edible chocolate brownie in my life, or so my family tells me, but the dogs love these things. Maybe they're more discerning and truly appreciative of my culinary skills.

Food Pans

My Dogbuddies and I don't all use the same kind of food bowls. You've probably noticed that I talk about "food pans." Mine are stainless steel, easy to clean, easy to stack, and easy to pack up and take along with us. My Dogbuddy Lauren, who is a world-class traveling companion, has a wonderful, ceramic bowl that has Jack's name on it. It is heavy and discourages a puppy from carrying it around and spilling a trail of water. On the other hand, my puppy's middle name must be "Water." He takes great delight in knocking his water over and trying to turn his immediate environment into a pond.

Maybe it's an old wives' tale, but it's my firm belief that plastic dishes can fade the pigment in the dog's nose. All I know for certain is that whenever someone asks about a faded nose, it turns out that his or her dog has been fed from a plastic dish. Don't apply logic here. In about fifty years, someone is going to discover that there is a scientific reason for this...a chemical reaction...something???

The Puppies

There are several schools of thought on feeding puppies. Here are the basics. If the puppy appears to be in slightly lean condition but is satisfied with his food, all is well. I look for a good coat, bright eyes, and a good attitude. The proof, as we say, is in the pudding. Well, actually, the stool. Gather round, we'll have a lofty seminar on the stuff. The stool should be firm, fairly dry, and well formed. It should not be a huge, sloppy, disgusting pile. Now, aren't you glad you're reading this book? You may as well know up front that this is what Dogbuddies talk about, sometimes over lunch.

I feed several small meals rather than one or two large meals. I can't stand the thought of all that kibble in a huge mass in my puppy's stomach. It seems as though it would be easier for him to digest a little at a time. For a long time, I give my puppies four meals a day. Breakfast, lunch, teatime, and dinner. Well, it's an English breed. What did you expect?

The Grownups

The Dogbuddies all agree that that grown dogs should be fed twice a day—morning and evening.

The larger breeds may be prone to bloat or torsion (when the stomach twists, in case you're wondering). Smaller meals with smaller amounts of water tend to help your animals to avoid this. A concentrated kibble is better here, too, because it doesn't swell up two or three times its size. Here's a little experiment. Put a few pieces of kibble in a pan of water, and go about your merry way for a while. Have a look at it later. If it has tripled its size, there is not as much food per chunk. Your dog would have to eat a good-sized pan of this dog food in order to feel full. The feed can soak up larger amounts of fluid as your dog is digesting it, and as it swells, it can create the problem.

My Dogbuddy Dr. Mary tells me that it takes about one and one half hours for the food to make its journey through the dog's system, so I give my dogs that much time before we engage in strenuous exercise. I also give them a chance to cool down after they've done a walk up, a double, and a blind. A five-course meal right after a 10K run might not be the perfect plan.

You Wouldn't Be Thinking of a Snack?

You already know that the Dogbuddies are going to have some treats ready for those little training scenarios. You call, your puppy comes flying, because he knows that a little "something" is on the way. Your puppy will do anything for a really good food reward. If you're a "cookie trainer" you'll use something soft, moist, and irresistible.

My Dogbuddies used to use hot dogs until they realized that hot dogs contain vast amounts of sodium. The puppies were trained in the evening. After all the salt in the hot dogs, they'd gulp down a bucket of water and then cry to be let out twelve times a night. Something had to give. It came to us that we needed a different treat. We call them Pâté Cakes. Later, we'll tell you how to make them. No, this will not be one of those well-guarded family recipes, so secret that it is necessary to leave an ingredient out. You can't ruin them. Keep them refrigerated or frozen. They're perishable. Now, don't you feel domestic?

But, I Think My Dog Is Hungry

So you've taken the best of the feeding advice. Your dog has been given his breakfast. He finished it off in about eight seconds. MORE??? You can't get away from him. He's watching you take a bite of toast. "Is that all there is?" He looks sad. Before you let even the dog make you feel guilty, bring on the snacks. A good, hard biscuit, a Kong filled with squeeze cheese, or, for the health conscious, some cut up carrots or apple. You're not sure your dog will eat them? It's okay. He can always have a lot of fun pushing them around the floor with his nose.

Final Thought on Food

Here is the last word of Dogbuddy advice on food. No one knows your dog as well as you. No one cares as much about him. In the ring one day, I overheard the judge, who was a very direct Englishwoman. She leaned over the slightly plump bitch stacked in front of mine and said, "Well, dear, you've spent a bit too much time next to your food bowl, haven't you?" The owner flinched. This is something you'd rather not learn in the ring.

But you don't need to worry. This is not going to happen to you. If your dog is overweight or underweight, you'll notice. If his skin is dry and itchy, you'll notice. You'll wonder about allergies and genetics. You'll worry about it all. And then, you'll do something about it. It will be the right thing.

Pâté Cakes

  1 lb. beef liver
  3 eggs
  1 Tbsp. garlic powder
  1 cup whole wheat flour
  ½ cup uncooked oatmeal

Process first three ingredients in food processor. Add flour and oatmeal gradually and process until fully blended.

Bake in 8x8 square pan at 350° for 20 minutes.

Cool and cut into 12 pieces.

Keep refrigerated or frozen.

10

Looking Calm or Something Close to It

You noticed that this chapter is headed LOOKING CALM. We are not talking about BEING CALM. My daughter Jennifer, who is one of my favorite Dogbuddies, tells me it is not how you *feel*, it's how you *look*. She definitely has a point here. You look calm and confident, and your dog thinks you know what you're doing. So does everyone around you, and that calm attitude is half the battle. This is one of those life lessons that Jennifer utilizes with the same ease in giving a major presentation as she once did in showing a puppy in Junior Showmanship.

All your Dogbuddies will recognize this scenario. You get to the test/show/trial/agility event, and you suddenly become a candidate for an anxiety attack. You're trying to unload, get set up, and get the dog ready. You feel clammy. You feel hot. You feel awful. Your hands shake. You have this terrible sick feeling in your stomach—really terrible. You wind up in the rest room with a lot of other people who are just as nervous as you. Why would a group of seemingly intelligent people subject themselves to this kind of misery? You could be doing something soothing like bungee jumping.

There is not one of my Dogbuddies who hasn't endured this fairly primitive means of torture. Why do we subject ourselves to this? Because we like doing things with our dogs. We're good at it. We feel good about ourselves when we achieve our goals. We're proud of our dogs, and we want other people to see them at their best. And the brutal truth: We are competitive people, and we like winning. We may not decorate our living rooms with our ribbons and trophies, but we want to be in the Winners Circle. At all costs? No. We love to compete, and we love to be successful but not at the cost of risking the bond of love and trust that we have with the dog. That's really why we're here.

So how do we get into such a panic? This is pretty obvious. We care. We're bright enough to know that we'd better take a look at what it is that is striking terror in our hearts.

Fear of Failure

You play it over and over in your mind. You clearly picture the worst-case scenario, and then you hit the rewind button and start all over again. It's like rehearsing for failure until you get it right. All right, I'm going to tell you right now that you are going to have days when nothing will go right. Your dumbbell takes a bad hop. Your dog has that perfect view of you from the corner of the ring. He heads straight back in a hurry, totally ignoring the jump. Isn't that what you always wanted? It is raining at an outdoor show, and the judge is dressed for it. Your dog decides that he is certainly not going to allow his body to be touched by anyone in a raincoat and hat. Happens somewhere every weekend. All that time, effort, and money, and the chance for a qualifying ribbon or points can be over in one horrible flash.

When I was in about the ninth month of a pregnancy, my husband offered to take our dog into an obedience trial for me. They came away with a first. He NEVER showed another dog, but from that day to this, he has taken great delight in stating, "I've never walked into a ring when I didn't win." My point here being? Show me someone who has never failed in a dog event, and I'll show you someone who hasn't been in dogs for very long.

One of my Dogbuddies tells me that there is a good reason for reviewing all these possible ways to fail. If you can imagine it, you can avoid it. I'm not sure about that, but it is a comforting idea.

John Wooden would tell his UCLA basketball teams, "Success isn't final, and failure isn't fatal." He would add, "It's courage that counts."

Fear of Looking Stupid

Now, we really have to deal with this. Any time you venture from the safety of your home in search of success at a dog sport, you court the distinct possibility of looking faintly ridiculous. Like failure, it is highly unlikely that you are going to die of embarrassment.

The saving grace is this. Every one of my Dogbuddies can relive, in virtual reality, the most humiliating moment they ever had, and it almost always has something to do with a dog. Hard to believe, but we get a perverse sense of pleasure in swapping these tales.

One of my favorites, probably because it didn't happen to me, was the story of the agility dog who was nearing the end of his run. Through the weaves. Perfect. Up and over the dog walk. Perfect. Only the tunnel and two easy jumps left. Victory was in sight. The dog shot into the tunnel and…nothing happened. Nothing. His owner called him. Clapped her hands. Nothing. Finally, she went over and knelt down to see what was wrong. There was her dog modestly peeing in the tunnel. This moment was not designed to elevate one's self esteem.

My Dogbuddy's first reaction was, "There must be something wrong." Not, "What a horrible dog." This dog was not trying to be evil. He had a bladder infection. Poor thing, he just couldn't help himself.

You can be so mortified that you crawl away and swear never to return. Not my Dogbuddy. She worried more about her dog than she did herself. She got to the bottom of the problem. After masses of improbably expensive antibiotics, the dog and she came back to play another day and finished a title with style AND a first place.

My Dogbuddies could try to forget these embarrassing moments, but it's more fun to retell them and make them a permanent part of our collection of hallowed dog lore. These nostalgic stories usually start out with, "Do you remember the day...?"

By the way, you may have noticed that I did not reveal my Dogbuddy's name or her dog's breed. I still want her to remember my birthdays.

Fear of Not Being Ready

This is one time where your well-honed sense of guilt and inadequacy can work to your advantage. I worry about being late because history tells me that it is a distinct possibility. In an enlightened moment, I came to the conclusion that getting there just under the wire might not be in my own best interests. I have run for airplanes and fastened my seatbelt just as the plane rolled away from the gate. I've slid into my theater seat just as the curtain was going up. In my present role as a grownup, I've decided that all that hysteria is just not fun.

Believe me when I tell you this. You will not miss your turn in Novice A. You will be ready when they call for Open, Dogs. How can I be so sure? Because I know how important it is to you. You are much too sensible to waste your entry fee because you couldn't get there on time. Judges wait for no dogs.

Necessity is the mother of invention. My son, Jon, who was once one of my fellow procrastinators, became a C.P.A. I guess that spending all that time with numbers did something to him, because now he is enormously punctual. He told me to try this. If I'm supposed to be somewhere at ten o'clock, I'm to tell myself it's actually to be nine forty-five. If I think I need six more months to complete my training for a Senior Hunter, I'm to give myself eight. It's tough having to learn these bits of wisdom from one of your children. I have this odd idea that I should have been the one to teach him that.

Imagine this. You have to be at the hunt test at eight-thirty. Your alarm is set for four-thirty A.M. You're awake. Of course, you're awake. You've been awake every hour on the hour ever since you went to bed. You get up and get ready as quietly as you can, trying not to wake the entire household. You move silently, doing your impression of a cat burglar. You make your getaway.

The sun isn't up yet. You have tea in your mug and Sting on the radio. Time is on your side until you try to locate the test site. Field events are usually held on large land grants located in remote areas. You can't decipher the directions. At dawn's early light, all the dirt roads "with the old mail boxes" look the same, and they ALL have old mailboxes. Okay. What's plan B? First of all, do NOT follow the car with the dog crates. They're lost, too. Return to the last place where you saw signs of human life, and ask for help. Ask someone with a gun rack, and generally they'll lead you to the place.

Though it may be a little challenging, you make it with time to spare. You'll always worry about being on time, and you'll never feel completely ready. But you will get there, and you will be ready. And the best part is that your Dogbuddies are there ahead of you, and they brought the donuts.

Fear of Making a Big Mistake

No one loves to make a mistake. You will spend a lot of time thinking of how a signal given too quickly or a whistle at the wrong time cost the dog his ribbon. Don't be too hard on yourself. Your Dogbuddies will tell you about all the times they did exactly the same thing. Just chalk it up to experience, and don't waste time assuming a ton of guilt. We all started in dog sports because we thought it would be fun. When the music stops, I get off the ride.

My Dogbuddy Mary is a veterinary neurologist. She deals in life and death issues every day. It has given her a sensible outlook on dog sports. "At the end of the day," she says, "win or lose—it's just a dog show. What does it matter?" Your dog forgives you your mistakes. As a matter of fact, he doesn't even mention them to you. Win or lose, he is the same dog you walked in with. You like him just as much now as you did in the morning when he jumped out of his crate. You need to let him know it. As long as you and your dog are on the same side, you can always fix the little things that went wrong.

The only time you need to feel guilty is if you have done something to hurt your dog. That is the biggest mistake you can make. If your dog can't look into your face with confidence you might ask yourself, "Why?" When you lose trust in the relationship between dog and owner, you have lost everything. On the other hand, when your dog's best reward—better than food or toys—is simply hanging out with you, then you know that you are doing something really right. Keep it up, whatever it is.

Your dog is the only creature alive who recognizes that you are the center of the universe. It's an enormous responsibility.

Coping

Back to looking calm: It all has to do with attitude. If you've ever watched a dance recital, (I'm an expert here; I've watched dozens of them.) you will see classes for the tiniest children. Their teacher has to coach them. They forget steps. Dancing together is, as yet, an unknown concept. Arms are up when they should be down, but they are having the best time. Making a grand exit, they leave the stage holding hands. The last little one blows a kiss. Mistakes and all, they think they are great. Their enthusiasm is boundless, and the audience loves them.

There is a bulldog that is the darling of the agility enthusiasts. I know that this dog was designed for other things, but someone forgot to tell her that. What she lacks in litheness, she clearly makes up in heart. She jogs around the course with breakneck speed, all things considered. She and her owner take such joy in doing it that the fun is contagious. She doesn't always have a perfect run, but that doesn't dampen her spirits a bit. She gets a roar of approval from the crowd every time.

Sure, we all know that even with great attitude, if your dog knocks off a bar, it's over for the day. But that doesn't ruin the day. You'll be back, and we'll be glad of it.

Keep Smiling, Everyone Will Wonder What You're Up To

Here are some tried and true tips for giving you the appearance of looking calm. Do you remember that show tune from the musical The King and I? Anna tells the children that to make herself feel brave, she whistles. She sings to them, "When I fool the people I fear, I fool myself as well." There's definitely something to that. If you can look confident, you can fool yourself, and that's half the battle.

When you get to the show site and you're unloaded and the dogs are safe and comfortable, hold a cup of coffee. I know you're too sick to drink it, but it looks very cool. You'll look like a pro at (yawn) just another dog show.

You walk into the obedience ring and after all that happy, happy, joy, joy, you start marching around the ring. You're barking orders like something out of boot camp. Your dog thinks that something is not quite right. He's beginning to worry about you. Lighten up a little. You'll both relax, and the judge will be relieved to know that you have returned from your out-of-body experience.

Deep Breaths

Now, about those deep breaths. Unless you're proficient in yoga, you may as well forget this part. Use the time to do something useful like removing the black dog hairs off your khaki pants.

Your dog seems quite cheerful, but since you are a mere mortal, you're taking this whole competition thing to heart. You feel stressed. This is how you tend to look at things…

All or Nothing Thinking

Everything is absolute.

> **You say**: The judge is going to hate my dog. The judge only likes Afghan hounds with a black mask. You don't actually know any of this for sure.

> **Your Dogbuddies say**: Maybe the last time you showed your dog she was what we fondly call "ugly months old," sort of a gawky adolescent. Maybe the last time you watched this judge, the best Afghan in the ring happened to have a black mask. You're going to try hard not to overgeneralize.

Jumping to Conclusions

You know how this goes.

> **You say**: I've never done anything in this building. I don't know why I bothered to come.

> **Your Dogbuddies say**: All right, get a grip here. Your dog is trained. He's ready. Maybe he'll win, and maybe he won't. Just like everyone else. When he ends up winning here, you'll decide that this is the best facility in the state.

Negative Thinking

> **You say**: He missed a weave pole twice yesterday. I know he's going to do it again. He used to be so good at it. He has a real problem with them.

> **Your Dogbuddies say**: Now, now. Let's look at the bright side. Usually he is weave pole perfect. He loves to do them, and once in a while he makes a mistake. I'll bet he doesn't have a problem today.

Head in the Sand Syndrome

Now here's a frame of mind we'll have to work on.

> **You say:** Yes, he did finish his Junior Hunter title in four straight tries. It was just luck.
>
> **Your Dogbuddies say:** Sure, there are some things at a hunt test that are pure luck. Like your dog's first water retrieve drifts toward him in open water. Everyone else's landed back in the cover. That's luck. Four straight passes? That's a talented dog with a good trainer.

Who's To Blame?

I have no idea why we all seem to want to blame ourselves regardless of whether or not we could have changed anything. I also do not quite understand why, on the other hand, we blame everyone in sight for things that go wrong. It doesn't seem to fix anything. In fact, it makes us feel worse.

> **You say:** It was my fault. I should have taken him out ten minutes earlier. Or, the steward didn't set my articles out right. The judge stood too close to my dog. It made her nervous.
>
> **Your Dogbuddies say:** Let's not worry about blame. You did a good job, and tomorrow you're bound to have a better day.

So What Should We Do About It?

One thing that I am really good at is LOOKING CALM. I have practiced looking calm for so many years that I have actually become calm. It can be self-taught. There are a few easy steps.

- Take real interest in the people around you. If you listen to everyone else's concerns, you won't have time to worry about your own.
- Identify your problems. Ask yourself, "How likely is this to happen?" and "Could I live with it?"

- Focus on the positive aspects of the day.
- Keep reminding yourself that you are a pretty decent person. Your Dogbuddies think so…and so does your dog. What better recommendation could you have?

Reality Check

Make no mistake here. Every day is not going to be perfect. This is the real world. Some days will be remembered as "the best," and there will be days that will be so miserable that you can't even talk about them.

One day stands out in my mind, and even after all this time, I can still remember every dismal minute. I had several dogs to show, and by the time I got to the site, the field was soaked from the steady rains we had been having. I parked as close as I could, but the grooming area was across a sea of mud—so was the parking lot and so were the rings.

I lugged the basset to the ring so he wouldn't get dirty. What a joke. When I set him down, he was up to the elbows in mud. The judge, looking for a place that was not under water, said, "Take him up and back." As far as I could tell, it was all under water. I took him up and back, and he splattered cold, muddy water all over my skirt—all over me. I lost. I proceeded to lose with every dog I showed that day.

At long last, it was mercifully over. I got into my van, and it was stuck, like the basset, clear up to the axle. It took a tow truck before, finally, I was able to drive home. I was wet. I was cold. I was grim. I was muddy to the skin. On the way to the kitchen, I stopped at the washer and started to peel off my clothes. My husband, having an analytical mind, discerned that I was not feeling conversational. He disappeared, and in a minute he was back. Handing me a bathrobe, he said, "I started your tub, and I left a Scotch up there for you." Years later when I was telling this story, my good husband asked, "Was that your husband or your lover?" It was both.

Every less-than-promising day I have, I measure up to the Day of the Mudslide. It makes all the rest look better.

The Other Side of the Coin

I've had many more good days with dogs than bad ones. My own dogs have done their fair share of winning, but my greatest win was with a dog who did not belong to me. Richard and Pat Norris of Champaign, Illinois, owned a flat-coated retriever they called Hulk. They had taken him back from puppy buyers in whose care he was abused so terribly that he was disfigured for life.

In an attempt to keep him from barking, someone had placed a wire around his muzzle. As it became apparent that the puppy was scarred permanently, the buyers had no further use for him. Dick and Pat reclaimed the neglected puppy and brought him home. They were told that he probably could not be saved, but stubbornly they nursed him back to health.

Hulk grew into a fine, upstanding dog in beautiful coat, except for the white scar that encircled his muzzle. When you touched him there, you could feel where the wire had bitten into the bone.

I was asked to show the dog at a national specialty. The judge was Mr. Ed Bracy, a well-known and respected judge. It was a large Open, Dogs class, a five point major.

Mr. Bracy came down the line and asked, "What happened here?" I said that the dog had been abused and was rescued by his breeders. The judge took the dog's head gently in his hands, and Hulk looked him in the face with his usual trust and undeserved faith in mankind.

"Yes, that's what happened. Someone wanted to shut him up." I moved the dog, and the judge continued down the line. Hulk made the cut, and I decided that the judge simply wanted to make the point that he would consider the dog despite the scar. It was enough for me, and Pat and Dick were delighted.

The scar, of course, was not the dog's fault. It certainly wasn't there to enhance his appearance. Judges had worried about placing the dog. There was some question as to whether he should be disqualified. At that time, he had not yet won his first point.

We moved the dogs again, and again they were carefully examined. Once more around, and Hulk had placed first in the Open class. When the other winners stepped into the ring, I knew that we were in very good company. Mr. Bracy again examined and moved his class and again had Hulk lead off the line. We moved past the judge, and he signaled to me and said, "You have my Winners Dog." As he handed me the ribbon, I said, "Thank you very much, sir." And Mr. Bracy said, very softly, "And I thank you. Very, very much."

It is the only day that I have ever cried in the ring, but my heart was touched by this lovely and courageous dog, his resolute owners, and the judge who recognized his worth.

Hulk, Ch. Sunshine's Tradewinds, CDX, TD, WC, went on to finish his championship easily in the capable hands of his owners. I was left with a perfect memory.

Waiting for the Good Times

DON'T get discouraged, and don't give up.

DO set up with all your Dogbuddies. They are the ones you'll feel like talking to if you have a disaster, and when you win, you'll need them for the celebration.

11

Show Time

Chances are you will see your first dog show on television or as a spectator. You'll wonder, "What's so tough about that?" And the answer is: everything. It looks so easy that it lulls you into a false sense of security. What could be so hard about running your dog around on a little piece of string and letting someone come up and pat him? Remember that I told you here: ANYTHING THAT LOOKS EASY IS NOT EASY.

Breeding Tells

Those beautiful Shetland sheepdogs you watch moving effortlessly around the ring did not get there by accident. Take a look at their breeders. You're looking at lifetimes of studying pedigrees and small fortunes invested in stud fees, entry fees, and show expenses. Even before that, someone was paying attention to bloodlines and the breed standard. To everyone's joy, they produced the puppy that you are getting ready to take to her first show.

You bought your puppy from a responsible breeder who recognized that your pup had "Show Potential." Since you no longer believe in the tooth fairy, you found it highly unlikely that your dog could make her debut without the benefit of conditioning, grooming, and training. From there, you began your search for the Holy Grail, a breed championship.

Oh, Happy Day

It's a perfect morning. You pull onto the show grounds, you're directed to the unloading area. You unload. You find a place to set up (hereafter known as your setup). You bring in enough equipment to fill the state of New Hampshire. You and your Dogbuddies have staked a claim in the grooming area, and your puppy is lying in her crate blissfully thinking about making her debut. You return to your vehicle, which, mercifully, has not yet been impounded, and you park it within walking distance of the building.

Now you are ready to get ready.

Hairdresser to the Stars

Grooming is a breed-specific art. What is correct for one breed is all wrong for another. You might get some clues from your breed standard, which you have already committed to memory. You study it now in the time you once spent reading John Grisham. If your standard states that the dog is to be shown in as natural a coat as possible, it means it. Let's not try to redesign the breed.

Your breeders may be your best grooming gurus. They want your puppy to look good, too. Their name will always appear in the catalog along with yours. Your Dogbuddies will pitch in, and even the competition might give you some hints.

Grooming is really calming. The dog thinks it's a form of massage therapy, and it gives you something to do with your hands while you're waiting.

I was once asked to handle a Samoyed at a Specialty and the day that followed. I had groomed and shown other northern breeds, but not that one. The Samoyed was given to me in immaculate condition, but I wanted to do her justice.

I came up with a plan worthy of a military strategist. I decided that I would set up near a very capable handler—near, but slightly out of her line of vision. As luck would have it, she was also showing a Samoyed bitch. In my stealth mode, I stationed myself close by to learn by example.

She put her Samoyed on the table; I put mine on the table. She mixed some cornstarch and water; I mixed some cornstarch and water. She applied it to the legs of her bitch. I did the same for mine. She carefully brushed out the coat on her bitch. And, so did I. She neatened the ears, and I neatened the ears. She painstakingly scissored a few stray hairs, and I found a few to scissor, too. She let the cornstarch paste dry. I let the paste dry. She brushed out the cornstarch until there was no trace of it; I brushed out the cornstarch—every speck. Her bitch was ready. Her handler slipped on her lead, and off they went to the ring. I was in hot pursuit.

The other bitch won on Saturday, but mine defeated her on Sunday. I didn't let on to my fellow handler until several show seasons later. Finally, I confessed. She laughed her head off and told me that I needn't have gone to all the trouble. I simply could have asked her.

What the Catalog Is Really For

It is a common fallacy that the purpose of the catalog is to list the dogs so that you can mark their placement or know who begat whom. It's a cover up. All your Dogbuddies know that you buy the catalog for one reason and one reason only—to scope out the competition.

Home Away from Home

Taking care of your dog on a show weekend is an altogether different proposition from taking care of him at home. He is confronted with danger at every turn, and it's up to you to keep him safe, relaxed, and cheerful. You've taken your dog out of his usual routine. There are too many dogs, too many people, too much fussing over him.

My Dogbuddy Sally, a professional handler, has a cardinal rule for the dogs in her care: The dogs come first. Their comfort comes first. They are kept safe and warm and dry. On a hot day, they have shade and plenty of water. We may have missed lunch, but the dogs will be fed before we have dinner. When we are tired and aching, the dogs will have one last walk. They are perfectly willing to play our funny games. The least we can do is to tend to their needs. Nothing takes the place of kindness.

Like young children, dogs are creatures of habit. They love routines. If you have read *Good Night, Moon* eight thousand times, you know exactly what I am talking about. Your dog has his own internal clock. He knows, with uncanny certainty, when it is time for breakfast. He knows his own crate when you travel. He thinks of it as "same house, different sky." He knows when to be ready for a walk and when to settle down and rest. He expects his biscuit at bedtime. He LOVES schedules. Stick to them, and you'll have a happy dog.

Armbands

The judge's valiant squire, the ring steward, dispenses armbands at the ring where you will show your dog. Give him your dog's number, and he will give you the armband. If you forget your number, ask the steward for a look at the catalog. You will recognize your dog's name. They'll think you're a little dim, but at least you won't have to go back to your setup to look up the number.

The armband is placed on the left arm above the elbow. It is a foregone conclusion that the armband fits no one. For you first timers, this is my best thinking on a proven technique for securing your armband. If you have a skinny arm, hold one end of the armband firmly between your arm and body. Double up the rubber band, which you found dangling next to your ring gate and put the whole thing around the armband. Do this quickly before the dog you are holding attempts to breed the bitch next to him. If your arm isn't skinny, use the rubber band on the little flaps at the ends of the armband. There is the distinct possibility that your circulation will be cut off, but you won't notice it until after the judging.

There. Now you and the dog are properly identified. If you are showing more than one dog, keep the armbands straight. You don't want to go into the ring with the puppy dog and discover that you have the armband for the open bitch. You don't want to do anything that could make you appear a) flustered b) inept or, heaven forbid, c) inexperienced. What is that about not having a second chance to make a first impression? Forget that. It's not a consoling thought.

Dressing for the Part

This is not a difficult concept. Your attire should be consistent with the required attire for the judge. Unless it is a steamy day, the male judges will wear a coat and tie. Gentlemen, that T-shirt from the Hog's Breath Saloon and the shorts you wore to mow the grass might not cut it. Yes, I do understand that they are both outdoor activities. Maybe you'd better consult with one of your female Dogbuddies. She'll be glad to set you straight. She's always glad to set you straight. Women judges generally wear neat looking sports attire—in workplace parlance, dressy casual. My women Dogbuddies understand this term perfectly. Now you're set, complete with pockets, of course.

Just in case you missed this the first time, SLOPPY IS OUT. It's a dog show. You signed up for it, you paid for it, and you are now in the public eye. Try on everything first. I'm not kidding here. It would be a shame to bend over in the ring and find that there isn't a way to stand up with all your seams intact. If you can't run, bend over, and kneel in your show clothes, you've got the wrong duds. If you're uncomfortable, you've got the wrong duds. Check the buttons and fasteners. Leaving items of clothing in the ring, literally, may not win you any points. At least, not from the judge.

Choose colors and patterns that compliment your dog. If you're showing a Dalmatian you might rethink polka dots. Try a color that sets off his coat. I recall seeing someone wearing a little

Scottish outfit showing a Scottie. It was just too much for me. But then, maybe they would have thought the same about my tweed jacket with my sporting dogs.

Think about the fabric, too. A nice backdrop for your dog? Sure. Miles of skirt? Well, if you are considerably more graceful than I am, you probably won't put your right knee on the hem of your skirt and then try to stand up. If your dress even remotely resembles a nightie, you might consider a slip. Now, don't make me go into this. Just think about it. Leave home anything that dangles over your dog as you are stacking him.

News flash! It's the dog that's center stage—not you. I was at ringside at a prestigious show where goldens were in the ring. I watched in awe while a *very* curvy woman in a T-shirt that clung like wet tissue took her dog away and back and presented him, along with all of her considerable feminine charms. The judge, known to be a very distinguished and courteous gentleman, was heard to say, "Uh, take him up and back again, and this time I'll watch the dog." Probably politically incorrect but, honestly, you could hardly blame him.

Professional handler George Alston, in discussing show attire, said, at one of his popular handling seminars, "The showring is not the place to make a fashion statement." It is a great place for a little common sense and some basic good taste.

Take a hard look in the mirror or at a photo. The camera never lies.

Show Shoes

When it comes to footgear, you will promptly discard any notion that your shoes will be an attractive addition to your outfit. Your shoes should have three important characteristics—comfort, comfort, and comfort. They should stay on securely when you are running. One of my Dogbuddies raced around the ring in a pair of mocs that must have been a little roomy. She seemed to think she was showing a racehorse. As she headed toward the finish line, she gave a little extra kick, and one of her shoes went flying into the crowd with the speed of a sliced golf ball. The next time she wore shoes that laced.

A Little Loving Kindness

If we're still talking about common sense and good taste, then I will broach one of my favorite topics: old-fashioned good manners. The ones we learned in kindergarten. Good morning. Please. Thank you.

It's easy to forget common courtesy. There's not enough space for the crates, somebody slipped into the parking spot that you had waited for, and you are almost decked by somebody who just has to get into the ring in front of you.

Frustrating, but the best thing to do is to respond with your customary good manners and a well-developed sense of humor. There are certain absolutes in the dog game, and one is that when you signed your entry form, you gave up your right to be discourteous to the judge. You also gave up the right to any display of unsportsmanlike behavior toward your fellow exhibitors, the ring stewards, and, most of all, your dog. This behavior should extend to the people who are selling catalogs and directing parking.

My Dogbuddies and I have a standing rule. It goes along the lines of the "if you can't say anything good about someone or their dog, don't say anything at all" philosophy. You never know whose mother is standing beside you at ringside, or whose breeder. So, don't say anything— until you're on the way home with windows up and doors locked.

Be careful. Word travels in the dog world faster than the speed of light. You mention that a certain dog has a couple of misaligned teeth, and in seconds, you are being quoted as having said, "That dog has the worst undershot bite I've ever seen in my entire life." You're quick, so you learn to avoid editorial comments.

Politics

Let's agree that we are all political. That's simply the human condition. Here's the big catch, though. When we are not winning, we look for someplace to lay blame. Our dog is perfect, so it must be the judge. That's it. The judge is POLITICAL. It is possible that the judge is political. But maybe, just maybe, our dog is less mature than or didn't move as well as the winner. Another *news flash*: The judge is not the enemy. The other exhibitors are not the enemy. The ring stewards are not the enemy. We need to look for the enemy within. We can concentrate on getting our dog in condition to win, or we can spend our time hunting for dragons.

The Plunge

It's time to head to the ring. The puppy is groomed to perfection. You have removed any chalk or powder from her coat. It isn't in your best interests for a cloud of white to arise from your puppy and land all over the judge's navy blazer.

While we are on the subject of powder, you may not have thought of this, but those of us with black dogs do not take it as a friendly gesture when the powder you are liberally applying to the white part of your dog's coat blows in our direction propelled by your gale force hair dryer.

You slip on your puppy's lead, and you make your way to the ring. You already found your ring when you went to get your armband. You may have noticed that nowhere in the rules does it say that Ring 5 is compelled to be next to Ring 6. One of the more complex activities at a dog show is comprehending the rhyme or reason of the layout of the show. Some clubs are kind enough to publish the layout in the premium list. Bless them.

You might be hyperventilating at this juncture, but I promise that you will still be breathing after you have shown your puppy and the ribbon is in your hand.

The judging, at this time, is divided by sexes, the dogs (males) first. Since you have a puppy bitch, you can stand at ringside and watch the classes ahead of yours. Purpose A is to understand the judging pattern. Purpose B is to give you a few minutes to settle down. Purpose C is to impress the competition with your calm attitude and beautiful puppy.

Am I in the Right Class?

On the day of the show, your puppy is the correct age for his class. Your Dogbuddies didn't let you make any mistakes when you entered. After a year, she will have to compete with the "big kids." You will notice that there are classes for Novice Dogs, American Bred Dogs, Bred By Exhibitor Dogs, and Open Dogs. The same thing will be true for bitches.

Later, when your puppy is over twelve months of age, you may think that she is not quite ready for the Open competition. You put her in the "also ran" class, Novice. Maybe I can hear from someone who will give me a really good reason for entering Novice other than "building" the points for a dog you have entered in another class. (This has been known to backfire, and the dog you put in as a "filler" winds up with the points.) Ever wonder why so few points are awarded to the winner of the Novice class? Since you know your bitch best, if you don't think she is ready, why on earth would the judge? After all, you ought to know.

Take Them Around

Puppy, Bitches, Catalog order. Words to strike terror in your heart, but if you are not ready now, you never will be. You check your left arm one more time and walk into the ring in the right place. Sometimes the steward doesn't ask for catalog order. It's more of a free for all, but you will get into the ring. Stay alert. Watch the judge. Watch the puppy. Your puppy is counting on you to do your best. No more time for nerves. This is the main event.

If you remember absolutely nothing else out of this section on show handling, remember this: HOLD YOUR LEAD IN YOUR LEFT HAND ONLY. If it is held across your body, you are advertising that you are a first time ever beginner. That may gain you a little sympathy, but not much more. Out the window will go all your attempts to look experienced. Again, repeat after me: LEAD IN YOUR LEFT HAND ONLY.

The puppies are examined and moved. The judge comes back to take another look. This is a great time to keep your puppy standing still. If she has never stood still in her life, this would be a really good time to start. Don't keep making adjustments. You set one paw; the puppy moves another. My English Dogbuddy Cyraine was judging Puppy Sweepstakes and was heard to say quietly to a nervous handler, "Loosen the lead on your puppy. You're hiding some lovely things about her." Left on her own, the puppy settled down and went on to take her class. Many times, the least handling turns out to be the best.

You are asked to take the puppies around one last time. The judge is about to make his placements. It gets tricky here. You keep one eye on the pup to make sure she looks her best and one eye on the judge. When he signals to his first, second, third, and fourth places, you are watching.

You find yourself standing in front of the big "1." Just as you planned it. Better than you planned it. You feel like Rocky. It is a great moment, and it's just the start. You're hooked. The judge checks your armband number and marks his sheet. You are handed the coveted blue ribbon, and you manage to say, "Thank you." For just a split second, you consider curtsying in the presence of royalty. Your fellow competitors congratulate you, and your Dogbuddies cheer. You, of course, take it all in stride. Your puppy gets a hug. You knew she had it in her all the time.

You go on to the Winners class. Maybe this time the Open bitch takes the points, but you know that, given time, your puppy will have her day. For today, her first ribbon is enough.

Photographs

You want to savor the moment, so you request a photo. When the judge has a few minutes, the photographer is called to the ring. You are told where to stack your puppy. The judge presents the ribbon for the photo, and the photographer asks you to make some minor corrections so that your puppy is standing perfectly.

Hope that your puppy is trained well enough to stand still. Judging schedules are tight, and the longer it takes, the more the judge might wonder why he liked this puppy so much. What was to have been a pleasant moment or two to have a private word with the judge can turn into a prolonged struggle. But not your puppy, not this day. She stands like the champion she is about to become. The photo is taken, and again you thank everyone in sight.

If it doesn't turn out quite that way, take heart. I had a very nice bitch who, as a puppy, was so wiggly in the ring we called her "the girl with the dancing feet." When she won her first major, I asked for a photo. The show photographer was the capable professional Earl Graham. By then, Abby's manners were faultless, so I stacked her and stood back holding her lead with great nonchalance, knowing she only required the minimum of control. Earl squeaked his toy and tossed it to achieve the correct alert show photo look. Somehow it landed in the next ring. Abby flew out of my hands, shot across the ring, jumped the ring barrier, and fetched up the rubber ducky. She came back the same way and delivered it to hand, quite pleased with herself. The judge, a very proper lady, was not amused. "Very unbecoming behavior for a show dog." When I regained what was left of my composure I said apologetically, "I am sorry…but it wasn't too bad for a retriever."

Bait

In your former life, bait was something to put on the hook to catch fish, but no more. That was yesterday. Now we're talking about a moist, chewy treat. Liver, in some form, seems to work best. It can be sliced and baked slowly until it is cooked through and dry enough not to be messy. Though liver, in any form, might make you gag, your dog will consider it the food of the gods.

Bait is used to get the dog's attention and keep it. It keeps his eyes on the handler, and it keeps him standing still. Some handlers hold it in both hands and let the dog pull off little bits. Some will put it in their mouths and spit out well-aimed pieces of it. I have always been of the holding school of thought as opposed to the spitting school of thought. It's entirely up to you.

The Dogbuddies suggest that you train your dog to bait just as you did everything else. Don't try this for the first time at ringside. The dog will be so crazy to get this terrific goodie that, in the ring, he'll be trying to tear your clothes off to get to it. I think you can live without the notoriety.

Kids at Dog Shows

My Dogbuddies and I generally agree that unless you have someone to give your young children undivided attention, they are better left at home. I see kids at ringside and kids sleeping at setups, and I'm sure that they have devoted parents who are able to show the dogs and know at every moment exactly where the children are. That was in the too-hard category for me. My kids stayed home with Dad until they were old enough to take care of me.

But that's for you to decide. Some of my Dogbuddies can do several things at once, and kids and dogs at the show create no problem. These are the same parents who can host a birthday party for twenty of their child's closest friends in the afternoon and prepare an eight-course dinner for the boss and his wife in the evening. I bow in admiration.

Junior Showmanship

If you think that taking one of your dogs into the ring is a heart-stopping experience, try watching one of your children take one of your dogs into the ring. Junior Showmanship can bring out the latent Little League parent in people who are normally models of good behavior.

The Junior Showmanship ring is run just like any other ring except that the young handlers are being judged on their skill in presenting the dog instead of the dog being judged on his conformation. There's a lot to learn here about dogs. There's a lot to learn in general about competition. Winning. Losing. Unfairness. Disappointment. Luck. Hard work. Victory.

My Dogbuddy Stephanie is one of those natural handlers, unless you take into consideration the hours upon hours she spent learning to look natural. The dog she shows in Junior Showmanship is not a campaigned show dog. Stephanie has trained her own dog from his puppy days. Her dog is groomed to perfection, and Stephanie is dressed for success. She doesn't do a stagy imitation of a good handler. She *is* a good handler.

Stephanie has learned what most of us know. When your mind is on the dog, it's hard to worry about yourself. When you see her in the ring, you know that she and her dog have formed a working partnership. His eyes never leave her. He was not always the poster child for Junior Showmanship. Stephanie's Dogbuddies remember when he would leave her and race around to visit everyone in her training class. But this Junior Handler has something in common with a lot of us. She doesn't give up. Winston Churchill must have known something about dog shows when he said "Never give up. Never, never, never, never give up."

Dog Show Food

You may as well know that nutritionists have been known to run, screaming in horror, after seeing the food that people eat at dog shows. If you don't start out with indigestion, you'll probably wind up with it.

There are several approaches you can take. First, you can bring a cooler filled with food from home. If you fit into the "better late than never" loading up category, however, you'd better skip this part, too. Food from home can be very comforting and, without much question, far more appealing than the food at the concession.

On the other hand, if you have a yearning for a good, old-fashioned "fat pill," then get in line with some of your fellow gourmands. You can count on a full menu of dog show classics: chili dogs, nachos, and that dog show favorite—Polish sausage with onions and green peppers.

Some of my Dogbuddies turn a nasty shade of green at the mere mention of food before the judging but eat like the defensive line for the Packers once it is over.

Other Dogbuddies get a cold drink but eat nothing until after the show. You'll find them at the nearest Outback. You'll be able to recognize them as show folks. They're the ones with the good-looking sports clothes and the ugly, but serviceable shoes, and they're saying something like "that bitch never loses." You can tell that the people at the next table with the four year old are NOT show people. They keep sending over outraged looks and covering their child's tender ears.

My favorite all-time food at a dog show was a Southern Cherry Nut Bourbon pound cake baked by my Dogbuddy Dee. We were there to try to finish a championship on Alexander, one of my dogs. He only needed two points, and I was hoping that this was the day. Early in the morning, Dee arrived carrying this spectacular cake. "This is Alexander's cake. We'll need it later to celebrate." Pure statement of fact. And we did. Everyone in the ring was invited back for cake. Nothing at a dog show has ever tasted so good. It's enough to have a Dogbuddy with that kind of confidence, but one who can bake and show dogs as well—now that's amazing.

Loading Up for the Ride Home

All of our children have traveled to shows with me. They've cheered me on and cheered me up. The eldest of our three, my Dogbuddy Jan, is called Planning Janny by her siblings. Do NOT ask me if I brought the right child home from the hospital. Jan knew that when I was finished for the day, I would go into a cool down mode, and it was almost impossible to get me to move toward home. Or move at all. You can be that tired. When she knew that I was showing my last dog, she would put everything away in the tack box, load the grooming table and chairs into the van, and meet me at ringside with the keys in her hand. Lord, I was glad I taught that girl to drive.

One last word on loading up for home. Check to see that you are going home with everything you brought. Some of my Dogbuddies helped me load up after a big show in Chicago. When I got about two hundred miles down the road, I asked where the tote was with all my grooming equipment. No one remembered picking it up. That is because no one did pick it up. We all thought someone else had taken care of it. It was left in the parking lot and was never heard from again. Definitely not one of my better moves, but then you do learn from these little setbacks… or you travel with your capable daughter.

Blinding Flash of the Obvious #2

- You are not going to win every day.
- You are going to win when you do not expect it.
- Winning is more fun than losing.
- Saving grace: The competition likes you better when you lose.

12

Love, Honor, and Obey

Somewhere after the Victorian era, brides, at least the ones who read *Modern Bride*, stopped murmuring the obey part of their wedding vows. Love and honor were fine, but obey sort of stuck in their throats. In fact, even children expect a rational, in-depth discussion when you ask them to take out the trash. Much work is done on an "ask me nicely, and I'll see what I can do" basis. So who's left to be obedient? The dog.

Welcome Home

You have a new puppy. He's sweet, and all you really need to do is to look after his physical needs. It's love in its purest form. Not many demands on either side. This is what you've been waiting for, but very soon there is a slight shadow over this idyllic scene.

The pup eats, grows, and begins to throw his weight around. He's jumping on you. Why is he doing that? Because he wants attention? Maybe. Because he wants affection? Maybe. But how about because you taught him? It's possible.

It goes like this. You call the puppy. You pat your knees, and he comes fast and happily and puts his adorable, little paws on you. You're so pleased to see him that, what do you suppose you do next? You pick him up—the biggest reward of all. A few weeks and fifteen pounds later, you are heading to obedience school.

Puppystart

This generation of puppy classes is different from its older cousins, the Puppy Socialization classes of, say, twenty years ago. Most trainers make good use of food and toys. The puppies have a really good reason to learn to sit, lie down, stand, stay, and come to you in record time. They most likely believe that if they're not swift enough in responding, the little Scottie will get the cookie. They toddle along next to you thinking it's a hoot to sneak those yummy treats out of your hand. Obedience is FUNdamental.

Before you start issuing commands that would make a drill sergeant proud, think again of your dog's extraordinary sense of hearing. In all due respect to collars, leads, and other training equipment, your voice and hands are the best tools you have.

Canine Good Citizens

Ask any of my Dogbuddies. Our dogs have to be responsible citizens, and we have to be responsible dog owners. Overturning trash containers, digging up flower beds, jumping on the toddler next door—none of these will instill love for your dog in your neighbor's heart. So you train a little more, and when your dog is a model of good behavior, you get him ready for an AKC Canine Good Citizen test. What else could you have done? The perfect standard poodle in class is being trained for it, and you have this overwhelming desire to keep up with the Jones's dog.

These tests were devised to recognize dogs who are enjoyed by their owners and not a nuisance to anyone else. All dogs, regardless of registration, or lack thereof, are welcome, and every dog who passes the basic requirements of good behavior receives a certificate. These are to be proudly displayed on the refrigerator door right next to "My child is an Honor Student at Newton Middle School."

Training clubs and classes offer instruction and sponsor the test. Canine Good Citizens can add their newly earned title after their names. When you fill in those forms at your vet's office, Sadie will be Sadie, CGC. Quite an accomplishment.

You Should Show Your Dog in Obedience

So this weekly hour of puppy training and your pride in your Canine Good Citizen thrust you headlong into a strange, new world. You learn the jargon. You win a little trophy at a match, and you know that you will spend the balance of your useful life in pursuit of green ribbons.

About a million years ago, one of my dogs won a homemade wooden plaque for a first in pre-novice. I still have it. It was my first happy experience with a team sport. My dog and I were the team. It was the only sport I had ever played where I didn't get picked last. I have spent the rest of my life being indebted to that dog. I am infinitely grateful that she thought that I had what it takes.

Trials and Tribulations

You need a certain temperament to enjoy obedience. You have to be willing to pay great attention to some fairly trivial details. At obedience trials, everything is about details. My Dogbuddies watch every crooked sit and have a sixth sense when it comes to understanding whether their dog is within a thirty-second of an inch of the correct heel position. Neither of these will cause your dog to fail, but they do make a difference in the score.

Obedience is exacting. Everything is precise and letter perfect. Along with all of that perfection, according to the rules, the dog has to feel good about his work. The AKC regulations state that "willingness on the part of the dog and naturalness on the part of the handler" is a big issue. To exhibit "willingness," your dog thinks of his work as a labor of love.

You need a split personality to really enjoy obedience. On one side, you are concentrating on quick, straight sits, and on the other, you and your dog are having more fun than taking the kids to Chuck E Cheez. Patty Ruzzo, a frontrunner in positive training, combines the precise demands of obedience with her own upbeat personality. Her dogs, Obedience Trial Champions, love to be with her. They would do anything for her. They don't care what she has thought up for them to do next, as long as they can be doing it with her. It would come as no surprise if she taught one of them to fly. She'd know the right spot to hold the cookie, and her dog would be airborne.

Take Thee to a Training Class

Not just any class. You need fun and games in the most literal sense. All work and no play make Jack a really bored dog. Boredom is the enemy of a great obedience performance. Does time stand still in the classes you're considering? A covert inspection should give you the answer before you sign up for eight months of them. Use your powers of observation. Ask your Dogbuddies. One of my Dogbuddies has tried them all. She is a dog training class connoisseur. Ask her.

See how your dog feels about it. If it's okay with him, it's okay with you.

Obedience Trial Duds

Once upon a time, obedience exhibitors dressed exactly the same as their conformation counterparts. Men wore coats and ties, and women wore tailored dresses or skirts. Somewhere in there, we had a fashion revolution, and pants became the norm for the obedience ring. Some say that the skirts got in the way, and maybe so.

Obedience then went through a "grunge" period where anything would do. The concept was that you needed to be in relaxed clothing in order to show an obedience dog. Interesting, because it takes more bending and kneeling and running in the breed ring, but let's not hamper any of this discussion with logic. Now, thankfully, obedience handlers, for the most part, are neat and attractively dressed. Why does it matter? Because an obedience trial is still an exhibition, and your half of the team is equally in the public eye.

My Dogbuddy Kathy always looks great, even at class. Her socks match her shirt. They're coordinated with her dog's lead. She's been a good influence on the rest of us. I asked her if she had been the Best Dressed Girl in her Senior Class. She was.

Obedience Grooming

I know that it wouldn't cross your mind to step into an obedience ring with a dog who wasn't well groomed. Your dog doesn't need to be in a show trim, but he does need to be neat and CLEAN. If the judge examines a Novice dog and then looks at his hands in disgust and reaches for a wet wipe, then everyone at ringside knows that a good bath was in order. Not an enviable position.

"Toto, I've a Feeling We're Not in Kansas Anymore"

You've left home and you've arrived in good condition at the fairgrounds/civic center/exhibition hall. Venues for dog events are all different, but they all begin to look alike. You find a parking spot and start unloading. This is where a featherweight dog crate comes in handy. You can carry it, along with your ice chest, chairs, and other assorted paraphernalia, in first and set it up in a fairly quiet place. Being a good day, today your Dogbuddies are looking for you and have saved some space.

This next is very important. Don't try to bring your dog in while your hands are full. It's hard enough to get him through the crowd, and things happen to dogs when we are not able to give them our full attention. My Dogbuddy couldn't see her dog over the mountain of stuff that she was carrying. Her bichon was your standard little white fluffy dog. Big dogs often think that dogs that look like this are wind-up toys brought for their entertainment. Her bichon ended up in the path of a playful and slightly out of control Airedale. He meant no harm, but it took weeks to get the little dog over her fright.

The message here: unload first. Then, when you can focus on your dog, bring him in. When you get inside, give him a few minutes to get his bearings. This definitely looks different than home. Settle him comfortably among his old friends, probably dogs he recognizes from class. This is a good time to get something cold to drink and have a look at your ring. Is there anything unusual that you might need to remember?

This may not seem possible, but I distinctly remember this episode. I was heeling a dog in a Novice class. It was in a large recreation room, and at one end there was a cold drink machine. As we made a left turn, a door opened directly ahead of us, and a gentleman in monk's robes stepped into the ring. He calmly put his change into the machine, took his Coke, and quietly left. My dog never missed a step. I decided that it must have been Divine Intervention. We had a qualifying score.

Are You Ready?

When you hear the words, "Are you ready?" you are off on another trip on Mr. Toad's Wild Ride. You are in the ring, and there doesn't seem to be any visible escape route without finishing the exercises. Your lungs feel as if they have been transported to the heights of Mount Everest. There is no oxygen, and breathing is no longer a subconscious activity.

Let me tell you about the time that I was judging Novice at a match. My next exhibitor came into the ring and sat his dog at the designated place. I asked if he had any questions. The answer was "no" so I asked, "Are you ready?" He nodded, but I noticed that he was pale and perspiring. Now, most of my exhibitors were pale and perspiring, but this looked a little different to me. "You are ready?" I asked again. "Well," he said, "in just a minute." He took a nitroglycerine pill out of his pocket and popped it under his tongue. "Now, I'm ready." I wasted no time. We zipped through the exercises. I wanted him out of the ring before he went into cardiac arrest. I went on with the assignment and didn't see him again until I was handing out the ribbons. He and his dog took a second. He looked a lot healthier. Maybe it was just pre-ring jitters, or maybe winning is good for the health.

Now you are in the ring. Your dog looks up, and you have been transformed into Captain Bligh—silent, terse, tense, barely saying a word. The dog wonders, "Whatever happened to my person? This must be someone they got out of Central Casting to perform the role of the OBEDIENCE EXHIBITOR." What it boils down to is that all this formality is scaring your dog to death.

Tough as it seems, you're going to have to let your dog know that this is all going to be fine, and in a minute there will be COOKIES. If your dog is in overdrive, slow down, and he'll take the cue. If he's worried and lags, walk fast and hope for the best. If you slow down when your dog does, he'll assume that he was right all the time. Between exercises, he could use a pat. In Novice you may guide your dog gently by the collar. It's a better idea to train him to walk next to you before you get to that point, but that's a matter of opinion.

Heel on Lead

That means a loose lead—no little tugs. There will be a couple of turns, hopefully not directly in front of the lady with the hot dog. There will be a left turn, right turn, and about turn. Under normal conditions, this is not too hard to execute, but under show conditions, I have known handlers to put a piece of yarn on their wrists to remind them. Hey, whatever works.

Figure 8

In Novice, it's on lead; forever after, it's off. Simple. Two stewards who, by the grace of God, will have no food in their pockets, will stand perfectly still and keep their hands out of the way. You and your dog will weave around them. The judge will call out a couple of halts, and you're on to the next. So far, so good.

Stand for Examination

If your dog has been trained to stand quietly when someone who likes dogs touches them gently, you've got it whipped. I should add that your dog's feet are to remain in the same four places that you left them. This will all go well unless your judge coos, "I just LOVE this breed." Then you're dead. We are going to assume that this will never happen, and if it does you'll get over it.

Heel Free

This is where we look for poetry in motion—dog and handler in tune with each other. Your dog is keeping pace with you step for step. Straight sits, eyes right. Your dog is convinced that it's worth it to stay close. No distraction can lure him from your side. The dumbbells landing in the next ring can't distract him. The shrieks of joy from two rings over can't distract him. Your dog is a wonder.

Recalls

This is easy. Your dog stays where you leave him. In Novice, when you call, he comes right now and sits in front. In Open, you can't make up your mind, so he starts off, he lies down, and then he does what you asked him to do in the first place, which was to come to you.

Retrieving

In Obedience, retrieving is for everyone regardless of breed. Dumbbells are collected from the floor in front of you and from over the solid jump. Your dog begins to wonder why you can't hang on to these things. No allowances are made for the fact that your wire-haired fox terrier is SUPPOSED to kill it before he brings it back. That extra shake costs a couple of points, but who's counting? (Besides the judge.)

Jumps

There is a solid jump, a broad jump, and a bar jump. Trained with some food and fun, your dog jumps with style. In Utility the dog is given direction, he is sent over first the bar and then the solid or the other way around. It really helps if he is paying attention. It also helps not to have someone behind you, outside the ring, pointing in the opposite direction at the same moment. But maybe these things only happen to me.

Stays

How could something so simple become so difficult? There is a rule of thumb that says that if your dog has performed all of the exercises successfully, it must be time to break a stay. My Dogbuddy Susan remembers leaving her retriever on an out of sight Open stay. When she returned to the ring, her retriever was sitting exactly as she had left him. She was really pleased until she found out that he had popped up and then sat down, all in a matter of seconds. What happened? It seems that when they were about two minutes into the stay, a pigeon swooped down over the ring. Understanding his real life's work, the retriever stood up for an instant to get a better look. Remembering what he had been asked to do, he instantly went back to his sit…too late. The answer? Train for everything you can think of, and expect the unexpected.

You will earn the affection of your fellow exhibitors by training your dog to be ready for the stay exercises when the judge asks if you are ready, not fifteen seconds later. Some handlers don't breathe until they hear "Exercise finished." You'd hate to make it any harder for them.

Articles

Think about this for a minute. In Open, you taught your dog to retrieve your dumbbell as fast as is caninely possible. Don't hesitate, don't deliberate, just fly out there, pick it up, and bring it back. And then what happens? Utility articles. "No," you say, "Don't just fly out there and pick up anything and bring it back. Hesitate. Deliberate. Just bring back the one I've touched." Your dog begins to wonder if he is ever going to get it right.

Signals

In the Utility signal exercise, silence is golden. My Dogbuddies do not utter a single sound from the moment the judge says, "This will be the signal exercise. Are you ready?" A verbal command cropping up in the wrong place would be fatal. We hate to be the ones to lose the points.

Directed Retrieve

Now this looks pretty easy. Three gloves laid out behind the dog. You turn and direct your dog to the one you want. The gloves are numbered 1, 2, and 3. The confusion lies in the fact that you are standing with your back to them, and in your somewhat altered state, it is hard to remember which is 1 and which is 3. Ah, well, practice makes perfect, or so my piano teacher used to say.

My Dogbuddy SueAlice is creative. Utility gloves must be plain white work gloves in proportion to the dog. She found tiny, white work gloves at Frank's and they are exactly schipperke size. Their actual purpose is to be part of one of those crafty gardening gift baskets. I wish I had been at Frank's when SueAlice explained how she planned to use those gloves.

Moving Stand

I have never been able to understand this exercise. If something is standing, how the devil is it MOVING? Semantics aside, you step forward with your dog and stop him as you continue to walk another few feet. When you have faced him, the judge, who could be the same one who "just loved" your dog in the Novice class, examines him and signals you to send him to heel. You do, and, wonder of wonders, he goes directly to heel without a front sit. Now, in Novice that would have cost you big time, but it is one of those little quirks of Utility.

Utility Is Never Boring

Say what you will about Utility (and some of my Dogbuddies have had quite a lot to say about it), it can never be considered boring. Your dog may come up with some really innovative ways of performing the exercises, and some of them may not coincide with the rules, but you know your dog is trying. A friend of mine, who is Irish, once told me, "God loves a trier." And we do, too.

Utility is not a good place for corrections. Every time the dog turns around, he runs the risk of making a mistake. You need to be so upbeat and have such confidence in him that you give him the courage to get through the whole thing. He keeps trying, and you are so pleased with him that eventually he puts it all together.

Obedience Trial Champions

These are clearly not your run of the mill dogs. Some exhibitors are content with earning titles with qualifying scores but nothing flashy. This is a matter of personal preference. I've had many Dogbuddies who took just as much pleasure in attaining titles as in being in the ribbons.

Some of my Dogbuddies marched to a different drummer. They worked a little harder. They set a higher standard. They competed a little longer, and the end result was attaining an Obedience Trial Championship. To do this, it is necessary to have a number of first place wins in the Open and Utility classes— not very easy, but if it was easy, everyone would do it.

These dogs are the elite of the obedience world. The best of the best are the ones who have earned Obedience Trial Championships along with titles earned in other aspects of the dog fancy.

Watch a few of these dogs. They'll encourage you to sharpen yours up a little.

Tracking

Tracking events are the competition form of search and rescue. They make use of the dog's natural ability to use his nose. The Tracking Dog follows a scent that can be anywhere from thirty minutes to two hours old. The dog puts his nose down and scents the trail through several turns until he finds a glove that was left by the tracklayer. Titles are awarded at several levels, each increasing in difficult. The good news is that you need only one pass for a title. The bad news is that while the dog can follow the track by using his nose, the owner doesn't have a clue as to where that glove is. You will be following along at the end of a long lead. If you are good at reading your dog and trusting him, tracking might be just the thing.

Rally

Rally is sort of obedience meets agility. It is not traditional obedience; it is not traditional agility but a combination of both. You and your dog move from sign to sign indicating the stations. At each station you demonstrate variations on heeling patterns, stands, recalls, and jumping. Events are timed, and handlers can talk and encourage their dogs. No touching or leash corrections. Rally keeps life interesting.

Obedience Has No Favorites

We used to hear a put-down of obedience dogs. Someone actually managed to say, "Well, if you can't show him in the breed ring, you can always show him in obedience." Maybe they meant that if the dog did not have the conformation to allow him to win in the breed ring, he could still be shown successfully in obedience. At least, that's the way I would put it.

Obedience trial dogs have some very remarkable characteristics. They have to love what they do and have the heart to perform some very exacting exercises under great stress. It takes a special dog and a special owner. Done right, it is beautiful to watch, the dressage of the dog world.

On certain days, my own dogs remind me of a note card I once received from one of my Dogbuddies. It showed two dogs out for a walk. One said to the other, "It's always 'SIT,' 'STAY,' 'HEEL,'—never 'THINK,' 'INNOVATE,' 'BE YOURSELF.'" Maybe some of that innovation would be a refreshing change.

There is no pattern for the perfect obedience dog or the perfect handler. It defies stereotypes. Take a look at the placements on any weekend. You'll see a Border collie placing next to a Dachshund. There are kids with their dogs and older folks with theirs and everyone in between. Many dogs are handled from wheelchairs. My Dogbuddy Steve is without sight, but he could see into his dog's heart and mind well enough to earn a CD in three straight trials.

My Dogbuddy Daphne and her Labrador demonstrate the results of blending training with natural ability. Sure, some dogs jump naturally and some dogs retrieve naturally, but no dog comes to obedience able to do everything naturally. I know that Daphne and Maggie have put hours into training, but in the ring it looks effortless. Maggie sits so quickly that her ear flips back, and she looks into Daphne's face with nothing but pure love. In my mind, THAT is the perfect obedience performance.

Blinding Flash of the Obvious #3

- Start your puppy's training between twelve and eighteen weeks. You don't want him to get the jump on you.

- Novice obedience is easy…when you're in Open.

- Open A was designed to torment you. Your dog thinks it's great fun.

- Utility is for Overachievers.

13

Out Standing in His Field

Along with the rest of my Sporting Dogbuddies, I knew that retrievers should have the chance to retrieve. It is their birthright. What I didn't know was that I would become the proud owner not only of a hunt test dog, but also a twelve-gauge shotgun, a case of popper loads and stacks of training dummies, a competition level duck call, and three different whistles, and that's just for starters.

You were ready to sit back and relax because for one split second you thought that this chapter didn't apply to you. Possibly, but if you have a spaniel or a pointer or a beagle, you had better deal yourself back in. If you have herding dogs, they can be in tests or trials, and it doesn't end there. You thought your borzoi was above it all? Your basenji too much of a free spirit? That was until they had a chance to do some lure coursing. Somebody told you that your black and tan coonhound was nothing but a hound dog? Your border terrier would rather be underground than above ground? Well, sports fans, there are field events for all of them, and your dogs are glad that you found that out.

Just when you think you might have a few minutes for an indoor activity, say balancing the checkbook, one of your Dogbuddies invites you out to give your dog a try in the field. Back in the shadows of canine history, dogs were bred to be useful to their people, who needed all the help they could get. Those characteristics continue to be crucial to breeders looking for the dual-purpose dog.

It's in the field that these dogs can prove their work ethic. Their pedigrees might not suggest an emphasis on work, and yet they can be as avid as their field cousins. Standard poodles are out there doing classy retrieves. It was only some of their humans who forgot that they were water dogs. These dogs were born to bring things back. My spaniel Dogbuddies demonstrate their little dogs' lightning fast whistle sits while the rest of us watch with envy. The pointer folks have cornered the market on control at a distance.

Keeping company with these dogs teaches you a lot about the awesome power of genetics. When that eight-week-old puppy is bringing you the sock, he's telling you something. He is asking you to give him a chance to do what he was bred to do. So you decide to get out there with him. After all, the exercise won't hurt you, either.

There is a field dog for all seasons. Some of my red-letter days have been with dogs in the field. Seeing them at work can give you some of the most soul-satisfying moments of a lifetime. It's hard to explain it to your non-dog friends over a candlelit dinner at an upscale restaurant, but it is true nonetheless.

Gearing Up for the Field

Only the gear that is needed for agility can outdo the gear that you need for the field, but, we'll get to that later.

My Dogbuddies, with their well-defined sense of competition, always strive to have the latest and best, a pursuit applauded by field outfitters everywhere. Some of the equipment is handcrafted, and some is manufactured abroad. Some of it can be found at your friendly neighborhood Army Navy Surplus Store. All of it has a price commensurate with whatever the traffic will bear.

Field gear can range from tiny, copper crimped blanks to SUVs that are capable of transporting an army. Whole catalogs are relegated to field equipment. Most of my field clothes are rugged enough to last through several generations of dogs. That could actually present a problem. It is virtually impossible to leaf through a catalog without finding something that looks better than anything you have. If you drop hints often enough in the presence of your Dogbuddies, one of them will buy it for you for Christmas, but, let's consider the bare essentials.

If You Want Anything, Just Whistle

We all have our favorite whistles. You must have more than one. When you settle on the perfect whistle, you will probably use it as long as you train dogs. Here's how it goes. You try out a whistle, and the dog comes to you and sits. Wow, this must be the right whistle. But one whistle won't do. Certainly not. All of your Dogbuddies have two on their lanyards. In case one fails at the crucial moment, you need to be able to reach for the second. Aside from that fairly unlikely possibility, the main reason is that EVERYONE has two whistles.

Regardless of distance or wind conditions, the dog can hear these training whistles. Actually, the dead can hear them. Some are made to project the sound forward to protect the field trainer's ability to hear, assuming, of course, that he uses earplugs when shooting and still has his hearing intact.

I use two different whistles. They are on a nice leather lanyard, but anything will do as long as you can reach it easily. I'll let your own personal taste be your guide. The first is a little British whistle with a high, shrill sound. It doesn't seem very loud, but maybe my dogs are paying attention. My second whistle is an Acme Thunderer. I use it for handling to blinds. In field jargon, a blind retrieve is a bird or bumper that the dog hasn't had the opportunity to see. The handler needs to guide the dog to it by the use of a series of sit whistles, hand signals, and the grace of God.

I feel compelled to say a few words here about the use of the whistle. Practice before you go out in public. Several short blasts are generally used to call the dog in, and one long blast is the sit signal. After a while, you'll get the hang of it. Probably after you've driven the family nuts, if not the entire neighborhood. Now, use some restraint here. If your dog is coming in to you at a good clip, you can stop whistling. He heard you; he's on his way. If you keep blasting away on that whistle, your dog really begins to wonder about you. He's coming as fast as he can.

Take the Labrador we watched coming in from a water retrieve. He looked like a small, black cigarette boat. It was beautiful, except for his handler's nonstop whistle. What more was the good dog to do? Walk on water?

So do your dog a huge favor, and use your whistle where it counts. It is a means of communication, and if you overuse it, your dog will begin to tune it out.

If my dog goes directly out, picks up the bird, and hurries back, I just wait. There is not much point in stealing his thunder. He's got it all under control. My biggest contribution is telling him, "Thank you, Alexander."

Herding handlers just smile at all of this. Their equipment consists of a crook and possibly a whistle. My herding Dogbuddy Bob tells me that he walks up to the post with the whistle he was born with. Herding folks obviously need very few props, if you don't count a flock of forty or fifty sheep.

Dummies or Whatever Falls From the Sky

Field trainers go nowhere without dozens of training dummies. People with boating backgrounds might call these things training bumpers. You see, they are the same shape as those things that keep your boat and the dock on a somewhat impersonal basis. Most of us call them dummies. Training dummies are canvas or plastic. Some look like a duck, but I don't think any dog has ever been fooled by one of them. Most people use the plastic knobbies as they are more durable; I prefer the canvas. My dogs are bred to be soft-mouthed, and I don't like to get them in the habit of picking up something hard. For as many who will agree with me, you will find as many who will not.

There is always plenty of room for an honest difference of opinion.

For puppies, there are puppy-sized dummies. Considering that puppies are capable of carrying half a sofa, they really don't require anything special in the way of dummies for very long. I do think, however, it is harder for a young puppy to deliver a wet plastic dummy without dropping it, so I usually stick to canvas. Try them both, and see what you think. One concept is universal. Keep your puppy training short and sweet. Retrieving is something your dog is going to do for his entire lifetime. We want to see him doing it with style.

Judges

Hunt tests, regardless of the organizations that conduct them, test the suitability of the dog as a hunting companion. Dogs are evaluated for marking, style, perseverance, trainability, and control. They need to be able to use their noses.

Judges have the responsibility of setting up hunt scenarios that simulate a true hunting situation. We've known a few judges who set up tests that are unlike anything any hunting dog has ever seen. You may as well prepare yourself for that. Some of my successful Dogbuddies tell me that they train one level beyond the level they are testing. For you forward thinkers, this is definitely the way to go. For the rest of us, do your best to get your dog ready, and then trust him to try to do the right thing.

Field judges normally have hunting experience and should always have dog experience. I've seen a few judges who confused the test with *The Weakest Link*, but, by and large, they are pulling for you and your dog.

Customary Hunting Attire

If you'll forgive me here, my question is, customary for whom? I have heard an ugly rumor that certain judges insist that the handler is attired in camouflage. Nowhere in any rules does it state camouflage as a requirement. I will go on record here to tell you that camouflage is NOT on my color chart. I hate looking like a pile of leaves. The rules call for "dark or customary hunting attire," and in my humble opinion, khaki or hunter green or sage is what they are talking about. British hunters for generations have worn their Barbour jackets and tweeds and Wellies, and they seemed to do just fine. Still, as determined as I may be on this point, I try hard not to be stupid. I do know who is signing the score sheet. At the start of each test, the handlers are called together for a briefing by the judges. If the judges ask for camouflage, I take out my one and only camouflage shirt and put it on. It's important to choose your battles.

Footwear

You need the right boots or shoes for the conditions. You will have your favorites. They'll keep you dry and safe. Soggy socks can really dampen your spirits. If you don't have a spare pair, check with my Dogbuddy Pat. She's bound to have an extra.

Shotguns, Blank Pistols, and Safety

From your puppy's early days, you have gradually exposed him to gunfire. First at a distance when he is doing something enjoyable. No mistakes here. It would be too easy to develop a gun-shy dog because someone wasn't thinking.

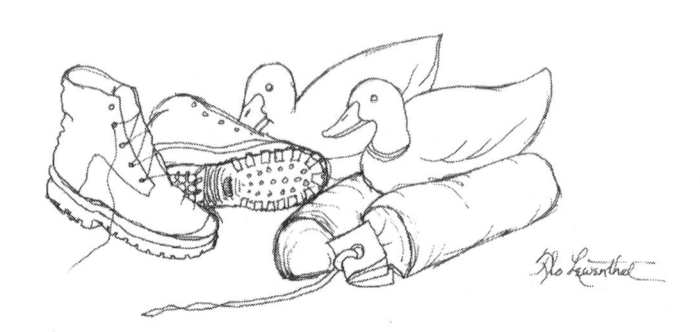

We use twelve-gauge shotguns and blanks in training to accustom the dogs to the sights and sounds of the hunting scene. They are always handled as though we have live ammunition. Both the poppers and pistol blanks can do real bodily harm if they are used without caution. If you have throwers helping, make sure that you teach them Gun Safety 101 first.

At a UKC test past the Started level, you will need to shoulder a shotgun and shoot popper loads (blank cartridges). You have to manage your dog, load and fire the gun, and remember to hand it back to the judge with the safety on and the breech open. Gun safety is a requirement of the test. If you find doing several things at the same time a problem, this could present a challenge. Take some time to learn gun handling from an expert, and make sure your dog is well under control. This is not something that can be left to the week before the hunt.

Duck Calls and Decoys

There are times when you will signal the bird boys that you are ready by using your duck call. You'd probably rather not sound like a dying duck, so like me, you could take a few lessons or buy a tape and practice somewhere far away from anyone else. My Dogbuddy Trey is a virtuoso duck caller. He says with a laugh, "Well, if my dog messes up, I can always wow them with my duck calling." He's got a good dog, and he can probably wow them on both fronts.

My Dogbuddies train their dogs on decoys on land first, tossing a dummy near them and encouraging the dog to be discriminating. You do not want to see your retriever heading back to you with a mouthful of decoy where the duck should have been. We are talking here, of course, about real working decoys—not to be confused with those beautiful, hand-carved objet d'art we have displayed on their own shelf at home.

The Field Trip

Going afield with your dog may not be exactly the same as a weekend at Club Med. Motels that accept potentially wet and muddy dogs are few and far between. Our all time favorite was a place that we will fondly call The Flamingo. There was some confusion about the keys as the owners had locked the office and had left them with a club member. We were handed one, but the room already had several residents who showed no interest in vacating it.

Our Dogbuddy Ann, who is a true lady, came to the rescue. The three of us shared her hospitality in a room that reminded us of a dormitory in an orphanage that had seen better days. Still, we were among friends and glad for a place to rest our heads. If anyone wants to swap tales of hunt test accommodations, we've got this one.

Field events are not for the fainthearted. You may be unfamiliar with the terrain. You may get a bad fall. Your dog may not have enough exposure to birds or water or gunfire. A lot of things can go wrong, but a lot can go so right that you'll be back again. Your dog is in his element, and that makes it a good day.

You may as well plan to be somewhat intimidated. Everyone seems to know what he or she is doing, and you begin to wonder what a nice person like you is doing in a place like this. At one time or another, all your Dogbuddies have wondered the same thing. Here's what you do: Concentrate on your dog. That will bring out the best in him. Help somebody else out. Look around. You'll find someone with far less experience than you. A word of congratulations or an offer for some coffee from your thermos may win you a Dogbuddy for life.

Dog 22 to the Line

You've been called to "get ready." This means that you can begin to hyperventilate. It also means that you have gone to get your dog, give him a drink, and walk him one last time. When he is working, you don't want him to stop for a "potty break." It distracts him and often takes him away from the area of the fall. You don't need him off the beaten track in search of the perfect, private rest room. Somehow, those little side trips do nothing to enhance his style.

You know that, at this point, there are two dogs ahead of you. Then, "Dog 22 in the hold." This is the holding blind where you and your faithful companion will wait to be called up for your turn to run. Awaiting the birth of your first-born child never seemed to take as long or make you feel as anxious. Finally, "Dog 22 to the line." You're up.

You may have noticed a few handlers being dragged to the line by out of control dogs. This is not a good indication of trainability. There's your dog walking quietly at heel. You both look good. You are finally on the line. You wonder why the gun stations appear to be in the next state. You are told to signal when ready. Your dog is sitting and waiting, and you are ready. You put one hand slightly behind you to signal.

Your dog marks the first fall and, in a moment of great calm, you wait to hear, "Dog." That is imperative at an AKC test. If you are at a UKC test, you will send the dog when he has marked the fall. Your dog leaves your side, and the retrieve is textbook perfect. You turn and once more your dog marks, takes a straight line to the bird, comes charging back, and makes a delivery that would make Fed Ex worry about the competition.

The next series goes as well, and you have a "Pass." You will want to thank the judges and give a tip of the hat in appreciation of those heroic bird boys who managed good, high, visible throws. The gallery gives your dog his earned round of applause. All's right with the world.

The Unconventional Wisdom

My Dogbuddies and I are now going to tell you some of our best-kept secrets. Don't give it another thought. We are here to serve.

The first of the Deadly Sins in the dog game is looking like a rookie. It can happen anywhere. In the showring, if you forget my valuable advice and hold your show lead across your body in both hands, you are immediately recognized for what you are—a first timer. There are similar pitfalls in the field. Stay with us, and we'll try to get you past them.

Ten Ways to Look Like Rookie of the Year

- **Make the test marshal search for you.** You don't really want to go there. The marshal's job is to keep the test running smoothly. No one else has the responsibility of getting you and your dog to the line. **Solution**: Your job is having your dog at the right place at the right time. Check the running order to see how many dogs are ahead of yours. When you are down to two or three, be prepared to take your dog to the holding blind. That means exercised and ready to go.

- **Try something new at the test; it might work.** Not a good plan. There seems to be a fatal attraction for anything new. This is not the moment for experimentation. **Solution**: Everyone around you will make suggestions. Some of them are useful; some are not. Go home, and if any of it still makes sense, you might consider giving it a try.

- **Refuse to recognize your dog's shortcomings.** You leave the line mumbling, "I've never seen him do that before." You continue training without altering course, and at the next five tests, he makes the same mistake. **Solution**: Back to the old drawing board. Back up to where he is successful, and then proceed with caution. We are all in a hurry, and the toughest part of training is admitting that we skipped some of the basics. Do not pass GO. Do not collect two hundred dollars. Backing up in your training is your fastest route to success. All training comes back to solid obedience. If you don't have a recall, you don't have a retrieve. (I've been trying to explain this small truth to my newest puppy.)

- **Tell your dog what you want the judges to hear.** Now, this one is going to do you no good at all. As you leave the line you say, conversationally, to your dog, "I can't believe you did that. You never do that in training. It must have been that bad throw." This invariably comes off as a self-serving excuse, which the judges have probably heard before. **Solution**: This is a good time to limit debate. If your dog flat-out fails, pick him up, (That, in field jargon, translates into "whistle him in, snap on his lead, and leave the line.") thank everyone, and make room for the next dog.

- **Conduct loud conversations when you are sitting close to the line.** Need we say more? Remember that this sort of thing comes back to haunt you. **Solution**: You won't want to be the cause of a bad performance. When you get to the line, you'll be grateful for the quiet.
- **Blame your dog.** We'll say it now. You taught your dog everything he knows. If he makes a mistake, take a hard look at where the fault lies. **Solution**: Give yourself a little time. You just MIGHT have missed something in the training.
- **Blame yourself.** Adopt an "I can't get anything right attitude," and soon you can't get anything right. **Solution**: You gotta believe. Sure, know what you need to improve, but keep all that self-doubt in perspective.
- **Keep changing training philosophies.** Now, that has to be designed to keep the dog confused. He never quite knows what to expect. **Solution**: Find a method that works for you, and stay with it. This doesn't mean that you don't make modifications. You do. But the Training Method of the Month plan is too unsettling.
- **You never taught him to be quiet in his crate.** The problem here is two-fold. First, you are making the other dogs crazy, and, second, your dog is wearing himself out. **Solution**: Take him home, and condition him to be quiet in his crate. It's not much fun spending time near a noisy dog—especially when it's yours.
- **Wear perfectly shined boots.** That's a total rookie giveaway. **Solution**: Get out often enough to gain a few scratches. Keep coming back, and you won't be a rookie, and you won't look like one either.

You can only be a first timer once. However, at any level in field eventing, you will have your share of defeat. Maybe you have had the worst weekend of all time. All you can do is try to take it in stride and file it under Lessons Learned.

The Work in Progress

While lure coursing and earthdog events demonstrate the dog's natural abilities, much of the other field events require a steady progression of work. Herding dogs have to maintain control of their fickle charges, and they need to maintain that control without any abuse of the sheep. These dogs require intensity and calm. That's a tough combination to have in one dog.

In retriever training, it is always a Brave New Day. You go to the field believing that your training has prepared the dog for everything. Guess what? That's virtually impossible. Some of us stay up nights trying to figure out what the next test will look like. We have seen all the test sites, we understand the inventiveness of the judges, and we're pretty sure we can picture the test. Where we got that idea I do not know.

I do know this. Field training is all about your relationship with your dog. All the training tools and gadgets in the world will not take the place of the trust and respect between your dog and you. They will not substitute for sound basic skills learned one at a time.

When we depend upon mechanics for punishment in the place of sound teaching principles, we begin to undermine our dog's faith in us and confidence in himself. And if we lose that, what is the real point of what we are doing?

All right, so when you sent your dog, he wasn't lined up properly, and you learned that wherever his head was going, the rest of his body was bound to follow. You made a mistake and sent him in the direction of the old fall. Oops. Well, you and your dog might make mistakes again, but chances are, it won't be that mistake.

Your Dogbuddies know that you are smart enough to learn from your mistakes and tough enough to try again.

Field List

- Lead and collars, slip lead, check cord
- Whistle and lanyard
- Extra whistle and lanyard
- Blank pistol
- Blanks
- Camo screen
- Knee-high rubber boots
- Duck shoes
- Socks
- Rain gear
- Change of clothes
- Hats, caps
- Bumpers, white, orange, canvas, and plastic
- Puppy bumpers
- Decoys
- Garden stakes
- Paper towels, wet wipes, toilet tissue
- Dog biscuits
- Other

14

A Leap of Faith

Take any agility event. You will see dogs having the best time of their lives. Their people are having fun, too. So are the spectators. That's why it's so appealing. It's a little like Gymboree for dogs, except that no one is singing "Jimbo the Clown Goes Up and Down." I do have a couple of Dogbuddies who would try that if they thought it would get their dogs around the course a few seconds faster.

I thought, at first, that it took a manic sort of personality to get a dog around a course. It might. You will bear witness to some sort of frenzy at the weave poles. You'll hear clapping, talking, encouraging, shouting, and imploring to help the dog through. On the other hand, when the dog jumps onto the table, he is flying high with adrenalin, and the handler stands motionless and fixated determined to keep him perfectly still. Agility requires communication and responsiveness.

As you watch your Dogbuddies in agility, you realize that there is some real magic to it. A movement of the handler's shoulder, and the dog slightly alters his direction to get a better approach to the tunnel. He responds to voice and body. The dog's superb reflexes make it easy for him; we mortals need to develop an exquisite sense of timing.

What does this remind you of? Well, it looks like a first cousin to equestrian jumping events. At last, a steeplechase event designed for dogs. Our English Dogbuddies thought it up, probably over a cup of tea. Dogs zoom through an obstacle course running full tilt against the clock—precision combined with speed.

Agility brings out the best in you. It takes the most positive of positive approaches. Here is a sport where you will be upbeat because it is the only thing that works. All dog sports have one common denominator—good total condition. Mind and Spirit. Body and Soul.

Conformation requires calm, efficient handling. Obedience is formal and precise. There is an exact format, which needs to be followed. In keeping with the hunting scenario in the field, handlers must remain quiet. Shouting is considered threatening. Do it, and you're gone. In agility, we have the other side of the coin. You will do whatever works to keep your dog buoyant and happy. And that's the operative word: HAPPY.

Agility takes confidence and a real sense of fun. So pack up all your cares and woes and let's try agility.

Hey, Look What's on TV

You were doing a little channel surfing, and you came across a dog and person running an agility course. What a pair! The dog was up and down an A-frame, through a tunnel, over some jumps, and through a chute in seconds. You thought, "Hey, my dog can do that." So you start thinking of adding one more piece to his repertoire.

Do We Have What It Takes?

Any sound and healthy dog can do agility. You understand, of course, that some breeds are more flexible and agile. Compare the bulldog and the papillon. They could be close to the same height, but the tiny dog can jump higher and run faster. The bulldog is probably wondering what all the excitement is about. Can they both do agility? Yes, but not exactly the same way. Can they both be successful? Just watch them.

And what about handlers? It might be easier for a marathoner like my Dogbuddy Bill. He gets around the course faster than some folks half his age, and he isn't even out of breath. Don't you hate that? We'll forgive him because he's such a pleasant person. If you aren't that mobile, you'll work harder on handling from a distance. Some of my Dogbuddies run the course from motorized wheelchairs. If you think for a second that this could be an advantage, try doing all your training sitting down.

All sizes, all shapes. They're all out there—going for it.

Like every other dog sport, you start with a little obedience. Your dog knows sit, down, stay, and when you call him, he comes right now knowing there is a treat in his future. He's got those things down pat. He loves to go for a walk and will even bring you his lead. He understands, "No pulling." He likes people and counts quite a few dogs among his friends. He knows that he has to stay in shape. Not to be outdone, you've discovered that agility has become the hottest new aerobic exercise. What better reasons do the two of you need?

What Kind of Stuff Do I Need?

In a moment of great madness, I decided that I wanted a full regulation set of agility equipment. The construction of this sort of thing is labor intensive. It has to last and be safe. All of this is reflected in the cost. I think I bought my equipment at a cost roughly the equivalent of a Jaguar. Maybe not quite, but, trust me, it's pricey.

And it takes up a lot of space—A LOT of space. I know you'll be relieved to learn that you don't need all of this at home. Start with a few PVC practice jumps, a plank, some masonry blocks, a set of poles, and a small tunnel. That should do it. When it comes to the large heavy equipment, understand that it takes three strong men and a boy to move it. Instead of owning it, head for your instructor's place. You and your dog can get the experience there, and you can rejoice in the fact that she made the investment.

However, as I hate being at a loss for items for you to purchase, I'll suggest one more. This will make up for keeping you from selling the family farm to buy the mega agility equipment.

What you really need is a canopy to set up at ringside. You provide your own shade and shelter from the elements at an outdoor event. These structures started appearing at agility events to keep dogs and people comfortable. Word spread, and now these little edifices, with their flags and banners flying, can be seen at most outdoor shows. Go to these dog events, and you think you're at the Renaissance Fair.

Who Knows Where and When?

You'll find several organizations offering agility competitions. In most areas in the United States, trials are conducted by the AKC (American Kennel Club), the UKC (United Kennel Club), and USDAA (United States Dog Agility Association). Each has its own rules. Just when you thought you understood the ground rules for one, you showed up at another organization's event, and it was all different—just to keep you and your dog on your collective toes. Back to the Internet to check the websites.

Sign Me Up

Your dog has a field/obedience/show title to display before or after his name. He has some manners and has stopped terrorizing your mother-in-law. Your family is glad that show season is over for a while and you might honor them with your presence at the school fair. And you do. But not before you check out the local agility club, and while you are there, you sign up for classes.

Your family now knows, without any doubt, that any hope that they ever had that you would appear to be a normal adult is lost. Possibly, if you have kids, they'll love watching you making a public spectacle of yourself. It will be hard for you to ask them, "Must you act so silly in public?" Silliness is sometimes a useful tool in motivating your dog, and a well-defined sense of humor is essential. This is a lot like teaching toddlers. You got your silliness experience while you were chanting, "This little piggy..."

Go to a class, and you'll have plenty of company. You learn as much from watching other dogs and handlers as you do from working your own dog. From the dog's point of view, agility can be a great diversion from other dog events. Your dog thinks you're talking his language. You can repeat commands; you can use your body to help guide him up and over and through the obstacles. You can laugh and encourage him, and your only correction is to try again.

It's so easy to see how positive training works here. Most of my Dogbuddies apply these same principles to everything they teach their dogs, and they have a closer bond with the dog because of it.

One at a Time

There may be no classes near you, or you might do better with one on one or small group instruction. One of my Dogbuddies described a class where she felt in the way and not experienced enough to be part of the crowd. Sometimes, that's just a matter of chemistry, but it's pretty hard to learn if you feel like you're at a seventh grade dance.

Find the right person to work with you. Find the right place. Maybe an indoor facility is better for you than out of doors. Maybe a private session makes better use of your time. Most importantly, find a place where both you and your dog enjoy the session.

Attitude Adjustment

You don't need a mood ring here. You and your dog can take one look at each other, and you both know what kind of a day it's going to be. If you're feeling really grim, I'm not going to try to talk you out of it. Go clean your desk. Put all of that negative energy to use. This is no time to be on your hands and knees inspiring your dog to come through the tunnel. Whatever you do, don't inflict that mood on the poor, blameless dog.

Agility is the place for energy and excitement. I have a slight problem with this. Maybe it's my body type. I was a tall, skinny teenager. The truth is, I was shaped a little bit like an ironing board. Curvy women were definitely in vogue. I had the same very soft voice that I have now. I was no one's idea of a cheerleader. It's not my normal style. But my dog knows me well, and he knows when I am trying. If he needs something more to help him to learn, I can outcheer the Dallas Cowboys Cheerleaders. All right, I can't look like them, but I sure can sound like them. If that's what it takes to keep your dog upbeat, you'll be cheering, too.

Basic Approach

My Dogbuddy Becky is an excellent instructor. Her own dogs are great to watch. When Becky works with us, she builds one skill on another. She's breezy and matter of fact, but she doesn't miss a thing. She is focused on quick responses in obedience so that you'll have those responses when you need them. She doesn't skip steps. If the dog seems uncertain, she knows that sometimes one step backward will become two steps forward. It won't hurt to hear again that in agility, as well as all dog sports, an attention to rock solid basic skills will save the day.

One of Becky's dogs is a rescue. She is proof positive that agility, in the safe hands of a caring trainer, can be a great confidence builder.

One early summer evening, Becky was working with us. On the obstacles that require a contact (the lower part of the obstacle that the dog must touch in order to remain qualifying), she had the dog hesitate with its paws squarely in the yellow part. To make sure of this, she needed something to put a cookie in at the bottom of the dog walk. It was a sure thing; I had every piece of dog training equipment known to mankind in my van. I said, "What do you need? I must have something that will do." Becky asked for a margarine lid. I looked blank. She said, "You know, a lid. Margarine. I Can't Believe It's Not Butter." I finally found something small and white but not a margarine lid. It was fine, but I was only relieved that my Dogbuddy Pat wasn't there yet. She would have said, "Let me look in my van," and the darn thing would have been there. Not that any of us are even slightly competitive.

As you can well imagine, I carry several of them with me now, but probably no one will ever ask me for one again.

On One Condition

We Americans are in the midst of a fitness craze. We are running, jumping, stairstepping, and weight training. We can't even pick up a magazine without being cajoled or berated into the latest exercise fad. Go on a cruise, and just try to float around peacefully in the pool. You'll find yourself in the middle of a group of other poor hapless souls being led in water aerobics by some lean, fit woman who looks great in her swimsuit. The only way to avoid it is to stay far away from the pool, possibly in the dining room.

We exercise to give our bodies their best shot at outwitting genetics and environment. Now that you are the proud owner of a canine athlete, you want to do the same for him. The risk of injury is far greater for the soft, out of shape pup whose only sports activity, until now, was the Twenty Second Empty-the-Food-Bowl event.

Your dog thinks he's in training camp. Easy does it. Conditioning is done gradually to increase strength, endurance, and flexibility. He'll be running at top speed, turning, twisting, jumping, and stopping on a dime. This will be easy for him if he is in correct weight and condition and thinks his work is play.

Know when enough is enough. Keep the jumps low and not too repetitive. It's the famous "one more time" that will do you in.

What to Wear

Here's where your Dogbuddies tell you to be ready to splurge. You need good running shoes. They need to have plenty of cushioning and plenty of support. They need to fit your foot. Your Dogbuddies might have a certain shoe that they swear by, but it might not be right for you. Explain to the salesperson what you will be doing, and get a recommendation. Everyone owns a dog, and your salesperson will spend a certain amount of time telling you about his or hers. That's okay. Listen and you'll be the favorite customer. The salesperson might even call you to let you know about the next big sale.

Dress comfortably in something you can run in. Pants or shorts are fine. Note here that "dress comfortably" is not spelled "come as you are." This is still an event that puts you and your dog center stage. Clean and neat are always in style.

I Think We Can, I Think We Can

You've put your folding chairs at the ring. Your dog is waiting in his crate, and you've picked up your number. It's exciting and fun, and, you can admit it to your Dogbuddies, a little overwhelming. You take a look at the Novice course, and every piece of equipment is familiar, but it is out there in a ring surrounded by, what appears to be, several thousand people. Just then you are called for the walk-through, your chance to walk the course with your dog and plan your strategy.

Your judge is one of those great, down-to-earth souls who seems to know that you are ready to self-destruct. She lets you know that she wants you and your dog to do well. There's no question, she's walked a mile in your running shoes.

You walk the course, planning the best angles to save time and the best approaches to the obstacles. You try not to think of the course as something with the complexity of the L.A. Freeway.

There are dogs running before you so, being a person of great good judgment, you settle down to watch. Oops, bad angle. Uh, oh. Wrong side. Ah, perfect, we can do that. You are a part of the applause for every effort.

Then it's time. Agility tests run smoothly with each dog ready as the last dog is finishing up. Your shoelaces are tied. Your dog is happy and up. Is he looking at you? Is he looking at that Jack Russell? No, he's focused. You're ready. You sit him. The time starts when he crosses the line. Is he behind the line? Yes. You leave him and position yourself for the first jump. Great!

We're Off and Jumping

The first jump, up and over. You've practiced jumps at various angles and distances; you're off to a good start. Your dog bounced over two bar jumps and flew over the winged jump and up and over the spread jump. Ok, now, the tire.

The Tire

Jump! He's through the tire. The A-frame is next.

The A-frame

All right now, this is his favorite. Up one side and down. Easy, easy. Watch the contact. We got the contact.

More Jumps

Come on, now. Jump. Jump. BIG jump.

Oh, Thank Heavens, the Table

Table! And Sit! And he does. That quick sit training comes through. And now, mercifully, you have five precious seconds to breathe. FIVE, FOUR, THREE, TWO, ONE and you wait for… AND GO!

And Then the Teeter

Careful, careful. Right up the middle. Please no sideways launches off the middle. And easy, easy. You're pleading. You've got the contact.

And on to the Tunnel

You're clapping and whooping, and he's through it in a flash. You're concentrating. What's next?

The Dogwalk

Almost there. We can do it! Walk it! And wait…easy, easy; get the contact. And only two more jumps.

Almost There

Jump! And jump! Don't hit a bar…it's too close to the end to hit a bar. Oh, please don't hit a bar. Whatever you do, don't hit a bar.

The Grande Finale

Chute! And he's through it. No refusals. No off courses. A clean run in forty-eight seconds flat. He's Tom Terrific, and you're pretty terrific, too.

Everybody gets hugs, and you know that you have done it. Will it always be as perfect? Maybe, not…but once you know you can do it, you'll be back to do it again.

And Besides Agility, There's Flyball

For those of you who can be content to let the dog do the running while you do the yelling, we have flyball. This sport explodes with excitement. Flyball was developed shortly before agility and has its own sponsoring group, the North American Flyball Association.

This would not be the sport for anyone who had taken a vow of silence. The dogs do the work, and the people do the shouting. It is a relay race, four dogs to a team. Each dog jumps four low hurdles and operates a dispenser to release a tennis ball. He catches the ball, turns, and jumps back. This all takes about four seconds. I can hardly take a deep breath in four seconds.

The competitive dogs jump horizontally, not wasting time with elevation. Different from an agility course, flyball always looks the same to the dog. He has two main jobs: taking the jumps and operating the box to get the ball— and all of this in record time. The skills should be taught separately. Think of learning to drive. You're just getting the hang of steering. You cannot adjust the radio at the same time.

Once again, we have a dog sport that benefits from positive training and good, wholesome fun. Yanks and jerks give the wrong message. Watch these dogs. What do they enjoy most? JUMPING. If the dog crashes into the jump and you call him away, it's not nearly as much fun as when he jumps cleanly and he gets to jump again. His biggest reward is jumping.

The Plus Side

There are national and international events in these sports. That's where the world class competitors are. They are the media darlings of the dog world. Most of us are not at that level. We are at the local events. No TV cameras. No breathless interviews. But when your dog runs the course and adds a new title to his name, he's the brightest star, and you wouldn't trade him for any dog in the world.

When you complete a course and your Dogbuddies watched your dog jump for joy, you might be remembering the timid puppy who was afraid to leave your side. You know what? You've got the true rewards of a dog sport.

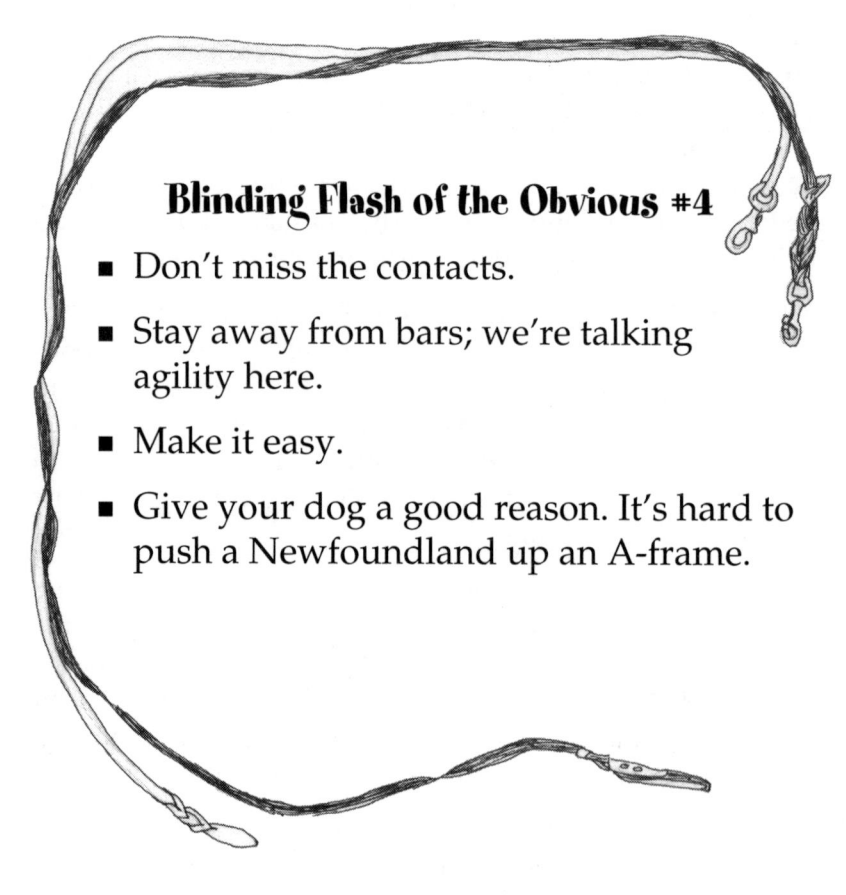

Blinding Flash of the Obvious #4

- Don't miss the contacts.
- Stay away from bars; we're talking agility here.
- Make it easy.
- Give your dog a good reason. It's hard to push a Newfoundland up an A-frame.

15

Remain Calm; Help Is on the Way

The worst reoccurring nightmare has been realized. Your dog calmly lies down in the last ten seconds of his out of sight stay in, woe is me, Open A. He aces his retrieve and then can't remember to come back. He says he couldn't hear his whistle. He took an easy win in his Open, Dogs class of twelve, and then he couldn't beat the puppy. NEVER MIND. You will both get past it.

- DON'T treat it like the tragedy of your entire life. Your dog is already over it.

- DON'T overreact to ringside advice. Everyone wants to help, but think about it for a minute. Even if it is well worth listening to, you are not in a good frame of mind for rational thought. As a matter of fact, you are not in the frame of mind for ANY thought at all. Wait until you get home, think it over, and then, if it still makes sense, act on it.

- DO remember that your dog, even your vizsla, can have a bad hair day.

- REALLY feel sorry for yourself for about an hour. After that, it's time to start getting ready for the next challenge. Your Dogbuddies can really be useful here. They'll tell you that it wasn't all that bad, that they remember a day when theirs looked worse, and then they'll ask you if you're ready for lunch. You are.

The First Step

The first thing to do is find it within yourself to congratulate the winner. This is a sport, and it is not without its protocol. Come on, now. Get yourself together, and offer a sincere word of congratulations. Maybe all you can manage is a word, but say it as though you mean it. This sportsmanlike courtesy lets you lose with dignity. It beats the heck out of storming out of the ring. Bad manners will not make you feel any better, and they will make you *look* worse.

Once in a great while, I can't quite bring myself to say, "Congratulations." We've all been there. In that case, I say, very courteously, "That was a nice win." (Now, don't start trying to remember if I've ever said that to you.) The dog world is a very small place, and you will be seeing these people again—probably next weekend.

Pay careful attention here; have a kind word and a pat for your dog. He did the best he could on that day. He needs to know that everything is still all right between the two of you. Don't take it out on him. That would be a BIG MISTAKE.

The Long Road Home

This is when you do your best Monday morning quarterbacking. You play it back in your mind. "I should have stood closer to (further from) the jump." "I didn't line my dog up before I sent him." "I didn't give myself enough room in the ring." There is no end to the self-doubts, and it is very easy to lose all the confidence you worked so hard to attain. After all, as you stepped out of the ring, some truly tactless soul managed to say, "It was all your fault. You should have..." You already knew that you had some responsibility here, and you didn't need anyone to remind you. Not then.

On the way home, you'll go over it with your Dogbuddies. You made a few blunders; the dog made a few blunders. You're even. By this time, you probably know what went wrong, and you know that there is a way to fix it.

Re-evaluate the Plan

Back on the day that you mailed the entry, you remember, there was this great sense of euphoria. You gazed fondly at your dog, and you said, "You are DOG. You are INVINCIBLE." And you believed it. Maybe your expectations were just a little unrealistic. Maybe. Maybe? Could it be possible that you took a few shortcuts? Too little training? Too much training? Give it some thought.

Maybe, in your concern over your Utility go-outs, you stopped worrying about your dog's signal exercise, and that's where he made the mistake. It's normal (I told you that I really like that word.) to concentrate on the weak areas. Well, now would be a good time to review all of your work and, this time, no skipped steps. Come up with a plan with some attainable goals, and work on it.

I Must Have Done Something Right

The mistakes always seem obvious. That's good, as long as the things that went well are obvious, too. Let's think, at least you didn't tell the judge, "But he did it perfectly at home." The one and only time I ever said that, the judge said, "Fine. Next time I'll judge him at your house." I guess he had heard that lame apology a few thousand times too many. Trust me, neither he, nor any other judge, ever heard me say it again.

Painful as it may be, we learn from our mistakes. Since you're still licking your wounds, you may not believe it, but it's true. My fourth grade teacher, Miss McGeary, told me so.

You get to take home the same dog you came in with. That's a good thing. And you get another chance. Every time you step back in the ring or out in the field, you'll be a little smarter and a little better prepared.

Your dog didn't bite anyone, and he didn't pee on the judge's foot. These things have happened. Don't you feel better now? A little?

Soul Searching

Still, on that awful day when disaster strikes you feel miserable. You feel disappointed, inadequate, and embarrassed. You begin to wonder what a nice person like you is doing in a place like this. Your mother always told you there would be days like this. How about whole weekends? You try to make some sense of the whole thing. You want some answers.

Why Does My Dog Do That?

You know that your dog can heel. He stays in the right position and gives you his complete attention, right up until you walk into the ring. Dogs do a lot of things simply because they're dogs. Maybe he needed to be taken to more places. Maybe he had never seen that many dogs and people in his life. Maybe he was scared or worried. Once you understand his problem, you can find the solution.

But Charlie Never Did That

Your first dog was perfect. He got all of your attention and time. He was the Wonder Dog. This is easy. So you started working with the next dog—same breed, same breeder, but an entirely different dog. What worked for Charlie doesn't work for Sam. He is his own dog. He has the same breed characteristic but with his own twist on them. So you make adjustments, and you fit your training to Sam's own individual personality and talents.

Every dog you own is not necessarily going to be good at everything. If you enjoy several dog sports, you will find that every dog does not have to do everything. Know your dog, and concentrate on what he does best. Some dogs are general practitioners, and some are specialists. It's your job to know the difference and to enjoy each dog for what he is.

But It Worked for the Other Dogs in Class

Right. But you don't own the other dogs in class. My Dogbuddy Nancy is a UKC judge and breeder. One of her breeds is the toy fox terrier. Her first TFT was Elvis. Nancy's training of this little dog had to be tailor made for him. He was a breed champion and a UCDX (United Kennel Club Companion Dog Excellent). Elvis lived past his seventeenth birthday. His progeny have gone on to great careers of their own, but Elvis is still the King. His training was scaled down to his size, but the end result was the same. You've got to know your dog.

Where Do We Go From Here?

United Airlines pilot Captain Al Haynes landed his crippled aircraft against terrible odds. In doing this, he saved lives that otherwise would have been lost. He believes that to avoid a disaster you need to have these five things working for you.

Luck

As in life, luck plays a part in any sport. Your dog is on a stay at the end of the ring, and the lady with the hot dog leans in to admire him. Your puppy misbehaves, except at the crucial moment when the judge is making her choice. The bird drifts into the clear, and it makes what looked like a hard retrieve incredibly easy. Someone said, "I'd rather be lucky than smart." How about both?

Communication

It's that two-way street between you and your dog. He's learning a lot of English, and you're learning a lot of Dog. Your dog understands your verbal and nonverbal signals. Keep an eye on him, and you'll know what's going on, too. Be sure you understand the judge's instructions.

In breed and obedience, watch the judge's pattern before you walk into the ring. Somehow, judges get really tired of repeating the instructions with every exhibitor. "A triangle, please." After the twelfth dog, it gets pretty old. You'll have the judge's heartfelt appreciation if you have been paying attention and act like you know where you are going.

Preparation

We're back to being ready. When you tell people you show dogs, they picture the seven glamorous minutes you have in the ring. Now, we all know that most of your time is taken up training, loading your stuff, feeding dogs, and walking dogs, all in preparation for the main event.

If you have a few minutes to sit down, you can watch training videos and read books to expand your knowledge of this magnificent obsession. While we are on the subject of books, find the books written for serious dog fanciers, not the copycat books where the content is exactly the same except for the breed of dog.

Attend seminars. They are given on everything from canine health to field training to handling. Your dog club or instructor will know about them.

My Dogbuddies and I have a Wednesday Morning Training Group. We learn from each other. We throw dummies for each other, and we go out to lunch.

Execution

It's great to be prepared, but at some point, you have to put all that effort to use. This is when you give yourself a good talking to. You settle down, focus on the job, and get it done. You'll stay on your feet, and it will all work just the way you planned it.

Cooperation

Cooperation is the final piece of the puzzle. You need the cooperation of the people around you. If you are not independently wealthy, you might need the cooperation of your employer. You can count on the cooperation of your Dogbuddies, but, then, they understand this whole thing. Depending on how organized you are, you might need the cooperation of your dry cleaner. Mine has been known to get my favorite pants done in record time.

With the Dog Sports Gods smiling, you will have those days when all of the parts of the puzzle come together. Let's hope it's soon and often. In the meantime, your Dogbuddy offers you half of a Baby Ruth. Maybe it isn't such a bad day, after all.

16

Letting Go

At first, it's just a little gray in the muzzle. Then, your dog takes a jump but with a little less of his usual ease. He still loves his work, but it becomes harder for him. You recognize these changes because there is not much that escapes you where your dog is concerned.

You are his protector, and no matter how important these dog sports are to you, they are not as important as the dog. When the time comes to retire him, you will know it. Your Dogbuddies have Senior Citizen dogs who still have the same energy and excitement about their work. If their age and health isn't creating a problem, then carry on. Some dogs mature later than others. Some reach their peak later, and some never seem to grow up.

Possibly there is a new puppy who is keeping a sparkle in your old dog's eye. You are glad for the addition, but you do not forget the dog who started you down this road.

You have fun with your dog in ways that are less physically demanding. You keep him healthy and comfortable. He's living out his life in the role of an elder statesman. You treat this dog in a way that makes sense for someone of his years.

Losing One

Members of my national breed club were given a survey on our dogs. One of the questions was "What do you like best about these dogs?" The answers were varied. Everyone liked their sweet and cheerful nature. Some liked their natural abilities. Some liked the versatility of the breed. The next question was, "What do you like least?" Again, there were many possibilities, until one of our members touched us with her answer. "Losing one."

There is never a good time to lose a dog. No matter how long we have with them, it never is quite long enough. When wrestling with the sad question of euthanasia, "Better two weeks too soon than a day too late," Joan Mason, a British breeder, believes. Often, the decision is ours, and it is our responsibility, as it has always been, to do what is best for the dog.

Will

The funniest dog I ever owned was Ch. Belsud Whippoorwill, JH, WC, a flat-coated retriever. He was also the smartest. He was the oldest here, so in the morning it was his job to signal that it was time for breakfast. At four o'clock in the afternoon, to the minute, he would let us know that he and his friends were ready for dinner. It was Will's greeting "Woof!" I would hear when I came up the driveway. When he was gone, his kennelmate, Alexander, took over his duties, although he had seldom barked before that.

Will was bred by Mary Grimes in England, and when I went to her home to choose a puppy from the litter, their sire was always sitting in the back of her Volvo station wagon. Just sitting. I thought at the time that it was pretty odd, but when I brought his son home, I soon found out that his favorite place in the world was, you guessed it, in the back of my van. If I left it open, he would jump in and wait for me. When he became very old, it was the place where he was happiest. I think Will was an optimist, and he always believed that there was a chance that we would go for a ride.

He lived until he was fourteen years and three months to the day. With our old dogs, it never seems quite long enough. My Dogbuddy Ellen sent me a note that said, "Will had a good, long life. He will be waiting in the back of God's van for you."

Your Dogbuddies know and love your dogs, and they are there when you need them.

And then you go on.

17

Getting on With It

You are having a great day; you are in the ribbons; your dog pins the birds; you placed in the group. It's what you worked so hard for, and you always knew it could happen. Now that it's here, it's your turn to be modest and appreciative. Of course. That's easy.

Or is it? While few love a poor loser, everyone vehemently hates a poor winner. Poor winners are in a class of their own. They can be readily identified.

All Over But the Shouting

It's your day. Your dog wins you a ribbon in obedience. That dog on the other end of your lead is the Winners Dog. Your dog has added a tracking title to his long list of credentials. You are ecstatic, but let's hold the brass band for just a few minutes. There can be such a thing as too much public rejoicing. Everyone cannot be a winner, and while you are overjoyed, there is someone who is disappointed. A little restraint here goes a long way.

The Arrogant Winner

You've seen this person. He'll tell you that, he "had the judge in his pocket." He doesn't acknowledge your congratulations and forgets that it was the dog who did all the winning.

Cheap Shots

This is the winner who downgrades the other dogs and exhibitors. As he leaves the showring he says, loudly enough for everyone to hear, "Except for him, there wasn't a decent dog in there."

The Real Winners

Mercifully, the poor winners do not make up the majority of dog sport exhibitors. It's far more commonplace to see winners accepting congratulations graciously. When you have had your share of both winning and losing, it is easy to remember how it feels both ways, and you take it in stride.

The important part of winning is that you are achieving your goals. When your dog has a major win or earns a leg toward a title, there is a real sense of pride and accomplishment. Your Dogbuddies, the people with whom you are the closest, have been with you and your dog on the road to success. They are part of your team, and they're delighted for you.

It's also nice to know that true dog people, in every aspect of the dog game, appreciate a beautiful dog or a beautiful performance. Your dog has well-wishers you never knew about.

Applause, Applause

We have a difficult time accepting praise. At the risk of a little sexism here, it has occurred to me that my male Dogbuddies are better at accepting congratulations than their female counterparts. You'll forgive me if I go out on a limb on this one, but it seems to me that when a man succeeds, he privately thinks, "Yes, I was pretty good out there today." A woman thinks, "Well, I got a little lucky." Maybe none of us accepts compliments very easily. It's good to be humble, but I draw the line at false modesty.

Remember, when you are being congratulated, it is not your responsibility to point out your dog's shortcomings. The only correct response to a compliment is THANK YOU.

I watched one of my Dogbuddies in the obedience ring. Her dog missed a few straight sits but otherwise did really well. As she came out of the ring, a spectator came up to tell her how great her dog looked. She smiled but she responded by saying, "Well, he had some crooked sits. It wasn't perfect." Her admirer looked a little embarrassed, as though he had missed some important points. Later, when we were alone, I told her that the kindest thing she could have done was simply to say, "Thank you." She accepted it as an honest suggestion from a friend, and we never mentioned it again.

Months later we were at a hunt test. My dog was fast and accurate, but just as I thought we were on the verge of success, he anticipated my "Back" signal to retrieve, and it was a disqualifying break. That brief lapse, in an otherwise good performance, brought our attempt for a "pass" to an abrupt end. His mistake went unnoticed, however, by most of the gallery.

I put the dog in his crate with a biscuit and headed back to watch the others. Someone was telling me what a beautiful dog I had and how well he had done. I said sadly, "Well, he..." and at that moment my Dogbuddy, of that obedience trial, caught my eye and was listening intently. In midsentence and without a second's hesitation, I continued, "Thank you so much. It's so nice of you to say so." My Dogbuddy grinned, knowing that she had caught me at the same thing I had pointed out to her, and on that day she saved me from myself.

Winning Isn't Everything

No, but as they say, it's a lot more fun than losing. On a day when your dog gets all his ducks in a row, figuratively or possibly literally, depending on your venue, your little corner of the world has a whole different look to it.

The judges are brilliant examples of fairness and wisdom. Your fellow exhibitors are fascinating conversationalists, particularly, when they are discussing your dog's virtues or your skills. The stewards or, in the field, the marshals are the very essence of helpfulness. And to whom do we owe this great good fortune?

The Dogs

First, last and always, it's the dogs. Only dogs could go along so willingly with the grandiose plans we have for them and do so well. Like the old Delta advertising slogan, they are "ready when you are." No excuses. No prior commitments, no important business in Tucson. They'll never tell you that they'll try to pencil you in. You are their top priority, and their top job is to make you look good.

The Dog Sports

One thing we have clearly learned is that there is the right dog for every dog sport and the right person. We can see that each sport is unique. All of my Dogbuddies do not need to enjoy all of the same events for their dogs. It's a diversity thing. One is not better than another, but one might have more appeal for you. Know thyself.

Mr. Jack Duignan, the AKC field representative for coonhound events, speaks with such enthusiasm about these dogs that I'm ready to pack up and go somewhere to see the hunt. It sounds as though they are held in the middle of the night and can last until morning. I might have to catch up on my rest the next day, but it would be worth it to see the coonhounds in action. At the very least, I'll rent *Where the Red Fern Grows*, and I'll be able to see a redbone tree hound. Jack discusses with me the differences in temperament and conformation of the various coonhound breeds with the same precision and passion that I would have in describing the five retrievers.

My Dogbuddy Bob, who started years ago in obedience with his bearded collie, trains for herding events. As he patiently explains the tests to me, I catch another glimpse into the many-faceted world of dog sports. I can picture the quickness and the devotion of these agile dogs. I can't, however, quite picture Bob with a shepherd's crook, so I'll have to go out there and see for myself.

Talk to these men, and their enthusiasm is contagious. Like most of us, they are generous in their willingness to share their knowledge.

The successful day you are having all began with something that caught your interest, and somehow it became a fatal attraction. It could have been golf or genealogy or kayaking, but it was dogs.

This is how it works. For whatever reason, you choose a breed of dog. You become so committed to your breed that every day you find yourself in a little deeper. You know more, and you become more involved.

What starts out as a pleasant pastime, becomes a full time vocation. What begins as a love for dogs, grows into a career. It might be in veterinary medicine or handling or grooming or judging. Maybe all you want is that welcome at the door and the moment of contentment as he rests his head against your knee. Maybe these are the biggest prizes.

We Never Doubted for a Minute

And here you are, in for the long haul. What once was a frightening, alien environment now is familiar, even welcoming. You're becoming an old hand. You've got the right crate and the right lead, and it doesn't bother you to eat your lunch on your grooming table.

That little puppy you started out with grew up and grew into the hopes and dreams that you had for him. On your part, it took a little courage and a lot of determination. Lo and behold, here you are in the winners circle.

You end up with the invitation to the group ring. You are enjoying bragging rights at the tailgate party after the hunt test. You're the one who can take a few minutes to console and encourage a newcomer. After all, not too long ago, you were a stranger here yourself.

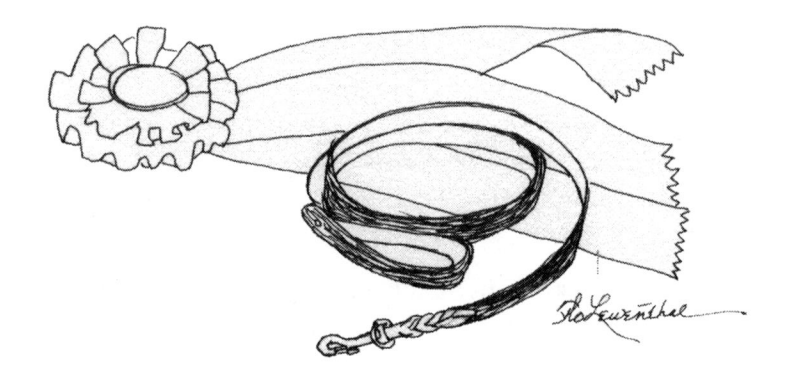

Postscript, Surviving to Come Back Another Day

This is what the whole thing is about—coming back another day. The dog game is the best of times and the worst of times, and you've seen both. Just when you're ready to call it quits, your dog does something great, and you're back at it again.

What makes it easier is knowing that you've got company. Your Dogbuddies are some of the best friends you will ever have. Hang on to them. They understand you, and, what is really heartwarming, they understand your dog.

You've had a great stroke of good luck. You share your life with a good dog who wouldn't want it any other way. Nowhere else will you find such uncritical love. Trust me on this, your dog will never notice that your show clothes are wrinkled, that you are covered in mud after his victorious water retrieve, that your nose and eyes are all red when he finishes his title. He thinks you look GREAT and…

So do your Dogbuddies.

Read On...

American Kennel Club. *The Complete Dog Book* 19th ed. Rev. New York: Howell Book House, 1998.

Burch, Mary R., Ph.D. and Jon S. Bailey, Ph.D. *How Dogs Learn*. Howell Book House, 1999.

Burns, David D., M.D. *The Feeling Good Handbook*. William Morrow and Company, 1989.

Deeley, Martin. *Working Gundogs: An Introduction to Training and Handling*. The Crowood Press, 1989.

———. *Advanced Gundog Training: Practical Fieldwork and Competition*. The Crowood Press, 1990.

Grossman, Dr. Alvin and Beverly Grossman. *Winning With Pure Bred Dogs: Success By Design*. Doral Publishing, 1992.

Milner, Robert. *Retriever Training: A Back To Basics Approach*. Ducks Unlimited, Inc., 2000.

Ruzzo, Patty. *Positively Ringwise*. Video

Savoie, Jane. *That Winning Feeling: Program Your Mind For Peak Performance*. Book and Audio, 1995.

Zink, M. Christine, D.V.M. and Julie Daniels. *Jumping From A To Z: Teach Your Dog To Soar*. Canine Sports Productions, 1996.

Zink, M. Christine, D.V.M., Ph.D. *Peak Performance Coaching: The Canine Athlete*. Canine Sports Productions, 1997.

Index

A
Agility events 127
   attitude 132
   conditioning 133
   equipment 130
   jumps 135 - 136
   shoes 134
Air travel 44
Armbands 86

B
Breeding 83

C
Canine Good Citizens 100
Cell phones 42
Choosing a dog 13
Conditioning 53
Coping 76
Crates 23

D
Decoys 119
Dog food 61
   designer dog foods 64
Dog Sports, conditioning 53
Dog treats 66
dogbuddy, definition xiii
Dogs
   and kids 10
   illness 49
   in advertising 10
   in entertainment 9
Duck calls 119

E
Euthanasia 148
Exhibiting 104
   articles 108
   directed retrieve 108
   figure 8 105
   heel free 106
   heel on lead 105
   jumps 107
   moving stand 108
   recalls 106
   retrieving 106
   signals 108
   stand for examination 106
   stays 107

F
Fear
   of failure 72
   of looking stupic 73
   of mistakes 75
   of not being ready 74
Feeding schedule
   adult dogs 67
   puppies 67
Fever 57
Field dogs 114
Field gear 114
Field training 23, 124
   dummies 116
   judges 117
   list of equipment 125
   travel 119

First aid
  basics 57
  eyes and ears 58
  overheating 58
  poisoning 57
  temperature 57
First aid kit, essentials 60
Flyball 137
Food, dog show 95
Food pans 66

G
GPS 43
Grooming, obedience 103

H
Health
  eyes and ears 58
  nutrition 61
  skin conditions 54
  teeth 56
  toenails 55
Heat exhaustion 58
Homemade dog food 65
Hotels 46
Hunting
  attire 117
  footwear 118
  safety 118

I
Illness 59

J
Judges 117

K
Kinds of dog food 62
  designer 64
  home cooked 65
  kibble 63

M
Manners 89

O
Obedience trials 101
Older dogs 147

P
Paw Laws 48
Photographs 93
Planning 29
  necessities 35
  re-evaluating 141
Poisoning 57
Politics, in dog shows 90
Premium list 16
Professional trainers 15
Puppies, feeding 67

R
Rally 110
References 157
Rookie mistakes 122

S
Search and rescue dogs 8
Service dogs 8
Shopping 24
  catalogs 25
  internet 26
  vendors 26
Show time 83, 90
  armbands 86
  attire 87
  bait 93
  catalog 85
  choosing shoes 88
  going home 97
  grooming 84
  junior showmanship 95
  kids 94
Skin conditions 54
Staying calm at the show 71

T
Teeth 56
Therapy dogs 8
Timeline 19
Toenails 55
Tracking 110
Trainers 15
Training 102
  puppies 100

Training classes 16
Transportation 34
Traveling 37
  by air 44
  food 40
  hotels 46
  in groups 43
  navigation 41
  partners 37
  Paw Laws 48
Trip planning 29

U
Unrealistic expectations 141
Utility 109

V
Veterinarians 51

W
Whistles 115
Winning 151